Soup and garlic cold fighters.
When garlic is cooked it is not strong-flavored
but sweet and soothing.

SWEET GARLIC SOUP

10 large garlic cloves, peeled, sliced thin (about ¹/₂ cup)
1 small onion, peeled and sliced into thin rings
2 tablespoons butter
6 cups chicken broth
1 tablespoon fresh lemon juice
¹/₂ cup croutons for garnish (optional)

In a heavy soup pot, sauté the garlic and onions for two
minutes until soft, but do not let them brown. Add the
chicken broth and simmer on low heat for 30 minutes.
Purée in a food processor; return to heat. Stir in the
lemon juice, cover, and simmer for another 60 minutes.
Serve warm with a few croutons floating on top.

Also by Eileen Behan

Microwave Cooking for Your Baby and Child
Eat Well, Lose Weight While Breastfeeding

MEALS THAT HEAL FOR BABIES, TODDLERS, AND CHILDREN

BY
EILEEN BEHAN, R.D.

POCKET BOOKS

New York   London   Toronto   Sydney   Tokyo   Singapore

Important: The author of this book is not a physician, and food or food therapy should not be used for the purpose of treating a childhood illness except on the advice of a physician. The information contained in this book is not medical advice, and cannot substitute for proper medical care. Consult your doctor before adopting the suggestions in this book or when your child is ill and in need of medical attention. The author and publisher disclaim any liability arising directly or indirectly from the use of this book.

The recipes for Blueberry Muffins—Hold the Wheat! (p. 157), Oatmeal Rice Cookies (p. 158), and Hearty Oatmeal Bread (p. 159) copyright 1985, The American Dietetic Association. "Food Sensitivity Series." Used by permission.

"Shopping Considerations for Special Diets" (pp. 151–54) was reprinted with permission from Kendall, P.A., "Managing Food Allergies and Sensitivities." *Topics of Clinical Nutrition:* 9:(3) 1–10, 1994.

"Hours of Sleep" chart (p. 203) from Ferber, R., *Solve Your Child's Sleep Problems,* New York, 1985, Simon & Schuster. Reprinted with permission.

An *Original* Publication of POCKET BOOKS

POCKET BOOKS, a division of Simon & Schuster Inc.
1230 Avenue of the Americas, New York, NY 10020

Copyright © 1996 by Eileen Behan

Library of Congress Cataloging-in-Publication Number: 96-17474
ISBN: 0-671-52986-2

First Pocket Books trade paperback printing September 1996

10 9 8 7 6 5 4 3 2 1

POCKET and colophon are registered trademarks of
Simon & Schuster Inc.

Cover design by Joe Perez
Front cover photo credits: *top,* Penny Gentieu/Tony Stone Images; *middle,* © FoodPix; *bottom,* Andy Cox/Tony Stone Images
Text design by Stanley S. Drate/Folio Graphics Co., Inc.
Line drawings throughout by Sarah Eileen McCue and Emily Christine McCue

Printed in the U.S.A.

*This book is dedicated
with great love and affection
to David, Sarah, and Emily*

ACKNOWLEDGMENTS

I would like to thank my mother, Elizabeth Behan, as well as Sharon, Sheila, and Kevin for their support; Trish Cronan and Brad Lavigne for their enthusiasm about the project; Judy Paige for her professional and maternal insights into feeding children, and now grandchildren; and Marilyn DeSimone and Madeleine Walsh for support, technical and otherwise. Thanks to the excellent staff at the Rye Public Library for helping me obtain hard-to-find references. My appreciation goes to Kathleen C. Bloomer, ARNP, and James A. Bloomer, M.D. for reviewing and updating the medical information in the manuscript. Thanks to my agent Carol Mann; at Pocket Books, I thank Amelia Sheldon. A special word of thanks to Emily Bestler for bringing this book to life.

CONTENTS

INTRODUCTION

When our children get sick, we want to do all we can to make them comfortable and to speed their recovery. Of course, there is no replacement for proper medical care, but for the majority of childhood ailments, the doctor will recommend only rest and proper diet as treatment. Many routine childhood illnesses or conditions, such as colds, stomach-aches, headaches, and sore throats, have no medical cures; for these conditions, food remedies are ideally suited.

Parents turn to food when their kids get sick because food can help heal an illness or relieve symptoms. Food remedies do more than provide nutrition. They offer comfort and they allow parents to participate in their child's recovery. Furthermore, food remedies have a strong placebo effect. If we believe something will work, it often does. This holds particularly true for kids. If Mommy and Daddy tell their 5-year-old that munching on saltine crackers will prevent car sickness, it probably will; it is impossible to sort out whether it is the crackers or the positive attitude that make the child feel better. No matter, as long as the treatment works and does no harm!

Today's parents get feeding information from the family doctor, a concerned grandmother, or even the popular parenting magazines. It is not uncommon to hear conflicting recommendations from these sources. I remember that when my children were very young, the whole family got sick with some sort of flu. Our doctor recommended that Sarah and Emily drink lots of clear fluids to prevent dehydration. Almost simultaneously, the media carried a slew of stories about the dangers of pesticides contained in apple juice, their favorite clear juice, naturally! Like me, our doctor was not well informed on this new issue, and briefly I thought I had to choose between dehydration or pesticide ingestion. I actually ended up with a suitable compromise of white grape juice and water for fluids, and soon the media informed us all that infant apple juice was virtually free of pesticides. More recently, milk, the food most associated with childhood, has drawn criticism. Some pediatricians have suggested it may be a cause of diabetes. When this news first appeared in the popular press, anxious mothers and fathers clamored for more information from their doctors.

Not only can feeding advice be confusing, it can be terribly vague. It's easy enough for the doctor to tell parents that their child should drink more or that they should make sure their child gets lots of calcium or fiber, for example, but it is not so easy for parents to actually put this advice into practice. Parents need alternative food sources to meet the desires of picky eaters and more details about the foods that are healthiest to eat.

I hope that parents will find in this book answers to the questions they have about feeding their children whether they are in good or ill health. My own children have experienced almost every illness discussed in this book. I am happy to say that with the help of the same information I'm offering you here, we have successfully nursed them through it all. If love is the best medicine, food prepared with love is a close runner-up!

1

SOLID BEGINNINGS

There are no single foods or group of foods that will prevent your child from ever becoming ill. On the other hand, good nutrition can speed your child's recovery from illness and may even reduce the number of times he does get sick. Nutrients are what keep your child's immune system functioning and it is his immune system that guards against serious disease. It follows that poor nutrition makes any immune system less effective. Deficiencies of protein, calories, B vitamins—even vitamins A and C—are known to impair the immune system's ability to fight off illness. It is impossible and unnecessary for parents to keep track of all the nutrients essential to good health. Instead, this book focuses on the nine I consider most important. They are carbohydrates, protein, fat, iron, calcium, vitamin A, vitamin C, vitamin D, and vitamin E. Foods that carry these nutrients also carry small amounts of all the essential nutrients.

THE NINE MOST IMPORTANT NUTRIENTS YOUR CHILD NEEDS AND THE FOODS THAT CARRY THEM

Carbohydrates: Provide energy (about half the calories a child needs each day should come from carbohydrate foods) and carry essential B vitamins, minerals, and fiber.
Sources: Bread, cereal, rice, and pasta group, including rolls, tortillas, crackers, cookies, rice, noodles, potatoes. Beans (also a good protein source), vegetables, fruit, juice, milk, and sugar carry carbohydrates, too.

Protein: Builds and repairs tissues. Makes up digestive enzymes and the antibodies that protect the body. Also provides calories for energy.
Sources: Meat, poultry, fish, dry beans, egg and nut group. Dairy products are a rich source of protein; grains such as rice cereal and bread carry protein, too.

Fat: Concentrated source of calories. Carries essential fatty acids and essential vitamins such as A, D, and E.
Sources: Butter, margarine, liquid cooking oils, cream, salad dressings from the fats, oils, and sweets group. Whole-milk dairy foods, along with meat, fish, poultry, and nuts, carry fat, too.

Iron: Prevents iron-deficiency anemia, essential to healthy blood. Carries oxygen in the blood.
Sources: Liver, red meats, poultry, shellfish, whole gains, beans; iron-fortified formula, cereal, and bread.

Calcium: Keeps bones and teeth healthy. Helps muscles contract and blood clot.
Sources: Milk, yogurt, and cheese group. Additional calcium sources include egg yolk, canned salmon with bones, dark-green leafy vegetables, soybeans, dried beans, and peas.

Vitamin A: Prevents night blindness, keeps skin healthy.
Sources: Vegetable group. Additional sources include liver, kidney, fish oils, milk, egg yolk. Carrots, sweet potatoes, squash, apricots, spinach, collards, broccoli, and cabbage all carry vitamin A in its precursor form, known as carotene.

Vitamin C: Enhances iron absorption; helps form collagen. May strengthen the immune system.
Sources: Fruit group and vegetable group. Excellent sources include citrus fruits, strawberries, tomatoes, potatoes, melon, cabbage, broccoli, cauliflower, spinach, papaya, mango.

Vitamin D: Works with calcium for healthy bone development.
Sources: Milk, cheese, and yogurt group. Sunlight, cod liver oil, herring, mackerel, salmon, tuna, and sardines are all good sources.

Vitamin E: Keeps blood, muscles, and liver healthy.
Sources: Small amounts of vitamin E can be found in all food groups. Particularly good sources include vegetable oils, wheat germ, eggs, meat, fish, whole grains, nuts, beans.

🦢 HOW TO MEET YOUR CHILD'S NEED FOR NUTRITION

INFANTS AND TODDLERS

The only feeding decision you need to make in the first months of your baby's life is whether to breast- or bottle-feed. Enjoy this time. Later on, meal choices are likely to become much more complicated! By 4 months of age, many babies are ready to start eating solids, though the milk feeding is still the primary source of nutrition. At this age, they have improved body control, can swallow better, and can turn their head away to signal when they are finished or disinterested.

When you start to add solid foods to your baby's diet, you will face new decisions that can affect her health. Dealing with food allergies, lowering salt intake, and achieving a balanced diet are all possible feeding trouble spots.

To reduce the risk of food allergy:

- Serve only single-ingredient foods; skip the combination dishes until your child is older.
- Introduce one new food at a time. Wait a week before adding a new food. If you suspect the food is causing a rash or digestive problems, wait a few weeks before serving it again.
- Cow's milk, eggs, nuts, fish, and shellfish are commonly identified as the source of food allergies. Do not serve them until your child is 10 months of age; in the case of cow's milk, wait until baby is 1 year old.

The taste for salt is an acquired one, and salty diets are linked with high blood pressure in adults. Studies show that when infants move from baby food to table food, their intake of salt skyrockets. Children eating a high-salt diet may develop a lifelong taste for salty foods.

BREAST OR BOTTLE?

Formula is not equal to breast milk in nutrition or the health benefits it can impart. Breast milk is perfectly designed to meet a baby's needs; it will even change in its fat and protein content to meet a child's growth and appetite. Studies show that breast-fed babies have fewer doctors visits and often recover from illness faster than formula-fed babies. Because a bottle cannot be propped or left in the mouth, a breast-fed baby is less likely to experience tooth decay from nursing bottle syndrome. Breast-fed babies are even more likely to have straighter teeth because the muscles that hold the teeth are better developed.

Besides the potential health benefits, breast-feeding provides secondary, psychological benefits. A breast-fed baby must be held to be fed, and Mom has to sit down five to six times each day to feed and cuddle her baby. This gives Mom time to relax and, most important, an opportunity for baby to bond with Mom. Mom can express breast milk so dad and other family members can participate in feeding.

Breast-feeding is not all blissful; it can be uncomfortable if breasts become tender and it means you are the only person who can feed your baby. Breast-fed babies are also notorious for waking up at night more often than formula-fed babies (thank goodness this is temporary). Despite these drawbacks, I would like to see new mothers breast-feed their babies at least for a short time. A baby fed breast milk for 4 months will be able to get many of the lifetime health benefits breast milk can provide. Today, 50% of mothers work outside of the home. Breast-feeding while working is difficult, but not impossible. There are many books on the subject. Contact the La Leche League [(800) LA LECHE] for information or seek out an experienced working mother for support.

DAILY INFANT AND TODDLER FEEDING GUIDE

These are general feeding recommendations meant to assist parents in planning healthy meals.

Birth to 4 months:

5–10 feedings of breast milk or 16–32 oz. of infant formula

4 to 6 months:

4–7 feedings of breast milk or 26–40 oz. of infant formula
Infant cereal (rice, oatmeal or barley) and infant juice can be introduced.

6 to 8 months:

3–4 feedings of breast milk or 24–32 oz. of infant formula
Strained mashed food, including cooked vegetables (avoid corn and peas), such as carrots and green beans, and fresh or cooked fruit are good choices to try now.
Try serving infant juices in a cup.

8 to 10 months:

3–4 feedings of breast milk or 16–24 oz. of infant formula
Serve foods mashed or finely minced.
Cereal and bread-type foods (2–3 servings daily): infant cereal, cream of wheat, oatmeal, toast, bagels, crackers
100% juice (4 oz. daily): orange, tomato, pineapple, or infant juices
Cooked or mashed vegetables (1–2 servings daily)
Ripe fruit (fresh or cooked) (1–2 servings daily)
Meat, chicken, fish, egg yolk, plain yogurt, beans, cottage cheese (1–2 tbsp. daily)

10 to 12 months:

3–4 feedings of breast milk or 16–24 oz. of infant formula
Serve foods minced or chopped.

Cereal, breads, all varieties of unsweetened cereal, rice, noodles, crackers, spaghetti (2–4 servings daily)
Vitamin C–rich juice (4 oz. daily): orange, grapefruit, pineapple
Cooked or raw vegetables (1–2 servings daily)
Fresh or cooked fruit (1–2 servings daily): ripe peaches, pears, and oranges are good choices.
Protein-rich food (1–2 tbsp. twice a day): lamb, beef, pork, fish, poultry, eggs, cheese, yogurt, beans, tofu, peanut butter

12 to 24 months:

Cow's milk and cow's milk products can replace some or all of the formula or breast milk feedings after 1 year of age.
2–3 feedings of breast milk or 16–24 oz. of formula or 2–4 servings of milk or other calcium-rich food: yogurt, cottage cheese, tofu, green leafy vegetables.
Cereal, bread, rice, pasta, noodles (4 or more servings about ⅓ of an adult-size portion)
Vitamin C–rich juice (4 oz. daily)
Vegetables, raw or cooked (2 or more servings)
Fruit (2 or more servings)—offer at least one citrus fruit daily
Meat, fish, or poultry; eggs, nut butters; beans; tofu (2 servings daily, each portion at least ½ ounce)

To control your child's intake of salt:

■ Do not add salt to baby food and do not serve processed foods meant for adults, such as canned beef stews, prepared soup, or frozen meals.
■ Avoid processed deli meats; serve plain chicken and fresh cooked meat.
■ Serve fresh fruit and vegetables and unprocessed snack foods or those designed for babies, as baby-food companies do not add salt to their products.

SALT

There is no conclusive evidence that salt is detrimental to children, but high salt intakes are unnecessary. Salt is a combination of sodium and chloride; it is the sodium part that affects body fluids and health. A high-salt diet is linked with high blood pressure and possibly asthma.

The addition of salt to so many processed foods makes the elimination of salt in cooking and at the table much less effective at controlling total salt intake than you might think. Children need a minimum of 225–500 mg of sodium per day to maintain health, and 2,400 mg per day is the upper limit. Studies show that many Americans easily eat 5,000 mg per day. The table below demonstrates how much higher in sodium snack foods are compared to most processed items.

FOOD	SODIUM (mg)
1 oz. corn chips	218
1 oz. pretzels	451
1 oz. cornflakes	351
1 cup pasta	1
1 slice bread	129
1 apple	1
1 McDonald's cheeseburger	672
1 cup 1% milk	123
1 medium carrot	25

Sodium cannot and should not be eliminated from your child's diet, but it is easy to see that she can get much more than she needs. Fresh fruits and vegetables are naturally low in sodium, dairy products are higher, and many of the foods from the bread, cereal, rice, and grain group carry sodium because salt is used in the leavening agents.

To keep your child's sodium intake low:

■ Do not use salt at the table.
■ Balance high-sodium foods with low-sodium foods. For

example, if you are serving a high-sodium canned soup,
serve fruit or vegetable sticks along with it.

- Read labels to learn which foods carry a lot of sodium.
- Choose snacks in the 100- to 300-mg sodium range or lower.
- Introduce your child at an early age to herbs and spices. These are wonderful salt substitutes. My girls help me grow and pick parsley, chives, rosemary, basil, and thyme, which we use in cooking.

Once your baby starts solid food, use the Daily Infant
and Toddler Feeding Guide on page 6 to guide you toward
healthy feeding decisions. After your baby's first birthday,
the milk feeding becomes less important (but not eliminated), and other foods must be added to supply the essential nutrients baby needs. A varied diet of all types of food
is what will keep baby well nourished. Milk can be an effective way to meet calorie, protein, and calcium needs, but
keep it in its proper place. Don't let a toddler substitute the
bottle for a meal. Milk is not a good source of iron or vitamin C. Don't serve low-fat milk until after age 2. Young
children need fat for proper growth.

Start a regular meal schedule and eating routine. Three
meals plus two or three snacks works well for toddlers.
Offer a spoonful of all the food groups at each meal, but
don't expect your toddler to finish what you serve—at least
not always. Serve snacks when she is hungry, but not as an
answer to boredom. Snacks should be low in salt and sugar.
Fruit, vegetable sticks, bread slices, crackers, even dry cereal are all good choices. In her first year, your child will
nearly triple her weight, but she can't continue at that rate
or she'll be as big as a five-year-old at her next birthday. For
this reason, children often eat less when they turn 1.

Toddlers are ready to feed themselves when they like
finger foods, want to try a cup, and practice with a spoon.

Learning to eat will be messy and time consuming, but meals are very important social events for kids, presenting an opportunity to express how you feel about food and your child. Make mealtimes pleasant and enjoyable. If your baby is spitting out the fresh green peas you prepared, don't get discouraged. A 1993 study in the *Journal of Pediatrics* found that babies do eat their vegetables eventually if they are repeatedly offered to them. In this study of 36 infants, it took 10 offerings before the majority of babies decided to accept the new, foreign foods we know as peas and green beans. If you have concerns about the type and amount of food your baby is or isn't eating, discuss your worries with his pediatrician. In general, offer a good variety of foods and trust your child. A healthy child will eat what he needs.

MILK: A TARNISHED REPUTATION?

Milk deserves singling out because it is such a prominent food in most children's diets and a swirl of controversy now surrounds it. Milk has been linked as a trigger in the development of insulin-dependent diabetes, identified as a cause of iron-deficiency anemia and food allergies, and accused of increasing mucus secretions during respiratory illness.

In response to the concerns about milk and diabetes, the American Academy of Pediatrics (AAP) convened a work group to look at the milk and diabetes connection in children. The annual incidence of insulin-dependent diabetes under age 19 is 15 per 100,000 persons. The work group concluded that avoiding milk protein in the first several months of life may reduce the later development of insulin-dependent diabetes. It is specifically recommended that mothers breast-feed for the first year of their babies' lives, particularly if there is a strong family history of diabetes. In infants whose mothers do not breast-feed, commercial infant formula made from cow's milk is the next recommended feeding. Soy-milk formula is not an accepted substitute for breast milk because in animal studies it, too, was found to be linked with the development of diabetes.

Another down side of milk is that it is a poor source of iron, and it can cause the loss of minute amounts of blood from the intestinal tract that can lead to iron-deficiency anemia. Cow's milk protein is also a common cause of food allergy when given in the first year of life.

During children's respiratory illnesses, lots of parents might withhold milk and dairy foods for fear of increasing mucus production. In 1992, Carole E. Pinnock published a study in the journal *American Review of Respiratory Disease* that found no association between milk and nasal secretions, congestion, or symptoms. She and colleagues objectively measured the nasal secretions in used facial tissues from 51 volunteers, most of whom believed milk would indeed worsen their condition, but no link was found.

The most recent milk controversy involves the use of bovine somatotropin (BST), a genetically engineered growth hormone used in dairy cows to increase milk production. Consumer groups claim that BST is not good for cows or people, but the U.S. Food and Drug Administration (FDA) disagrees and has approved its use. According to the FDA, there are no known health reasons not to drink milk that comes from treated cows—and it looks and tastes just like any milk.

With all the concern regarding milk, one might ask why milk should be included at all. Milk is still being recommended for children because of the nutrients it does contain. Milk, along with other dairy products, such as cheese and yogurt, is preferred by most kids over other calcium-rich foods, such as beans and green leafy vegetables. Just 1 cup carries 25% of the U.S. Recommended Daily Allowance (RDA) for calcium, and it is a great source of protein and riboflavin and is fortified with vitamin D. Raw milk is not necessarily organic and it is not recommended for children because it can contain harmful bacteria—serve only pasteurized milk.

OLDER CHILDREN

As your child gets older and breast milk or formula no longer makes up the bulk of his diet, balanced eating becomes more important. There is no one food that your child must eat to be healthy but he does need to get enough of the foods that carry the essential nutrients. To make nutrition and meal planning simpler, parents can turn to the Food Guide Pyramid (see page 16). The pyramid follows the Dietary Guidelines for Americans—guidelines for a healthful diet for Americans 2 years of age or older. The Food Guide Pyramid replaces the old four food groups that most of us learned about when we were in high school. The pyramid represents what the total diet should look like and it addresses overnutrition in addition to undernutrition. The key points to remember about the Food Guide are:

- *Variety:* Parents should offer a wide variety of foods to children.
- *Moderation:* The suggested number and size of servings are good guides for balanced nutrition.
- *Proportionality:* Serve more foods from the larger groups and fewer from the smaller ones.

To use the pyramid, start at the base; bread, cereal, rice and pasta should form the foundation of your child's menu. These are the complex-carbohydrate foods. Notice that the vegetable group is larger than the fruit group. Vegetables carry lots of minerals and vitamins; fruits carry mostly vitamins. To meet calcium needs, your child should always eat at least the minimum two servings from the milk, yogurt, and cheese group. Two servings from the meat, poultry, fish, dry beans, eggs, and nuts group will meet your child's need for protein.

FOUR WAYS TO MAKE FAMILY MEALS HEALTHIER AND COOKING EASIER

1. Start the day off right! Serve at least two fruits at breakfast, such as a glass of juice and a banana, grapefruit, or melon. Serve whole-grain cereal, toast, or bagels.
2. At lunch and supper, be alert to ways to add veggies. Try a grated-carrot salad, add tomatoes to a sandwich, or fortify a soup with minced vegetables.
3. Plan meals by making use of the Food Guide Pyramid (see page 16). Think of the bread, cereal, rice, and pasta group as the main course in your menu. Make foods from the meat, poultry, fish, dry beans, and egg group the side dish.
4. To make life easier, keep precut, washed vegetables on hand and canned no-added-sugar fruits. Stock the cupboard with canned ready-to-use beans for chilies, soups, and stews.

REALLY GOOD FOODS FOR YOUR KIDS

There is no one perfect food. Any food that comes to us unprocessed and unrefined is likely to be packed with nutrients and good for kids. There are some foods that are particularly rich in specific nutrients and chemicals that may be beneficial to your child's health. Don't force your child to eat any of these foods if he doesn't want to, but consider these as snacks or part of meals when you're deciding what to feed him.

Yogurt, Mother Nature's Penicillin?

Yogurt is not a substitute for antibiotics, but it might be useful when they are prescribed. Yogurt is a good source of protein and carbohydrate nutrients that may be able to counter the side effects of diarrhea and stomachaches that can come with these medicines. Serve yogurt when the doctor or pharmacist says to take medication with food. Antibiotic therapy can disrupt the friendly healthy bacteria that live in the intestine. Yogurt made with live cultures may restore or maintain the bacterial balance in your child's intestinal tract, and studies show that yogurt cultures can help control infection. To get the most health-promoting yogurt, look for one with a label noting that it contains live cultures. Heat-treating yogurt prolongs shelf life, but beneficial cultures can be destroyed by this process.

Foodaceuticals?

There are hundreds—maybe thousands—of chemicals found in plants that go by the collective name *phytochemicals*, and they may be the reason why people who eat their fruits and vegetables have less cancer. All the cruciferous vegetables, such as Brussels sprouts, cabbage, cauliflower, broccoli, turnips, and rutabagas, carry a variety of these health-promoting chemicals. Many varieties of fruit carry ferulic acid, which may bind with nitrates to prevent them from turning into cancer-causing nitrosamines. Grapes are a great source of the phytochemical known as ellagic acid. Soybeans carry lots of these plant chemicals, too. In short, the whole plant kingdom, from apples to zucchini, is packed with them. To give potential cancer-prevention benefits to your children, offer them a wide variety of fruits and veggies and encourage them to eat the minimum servings of these foods suggested in the Food Guide Pyramid (see page 16).

Fish

Serve fish a few times a week, and there is a very good chance you will reduce your child's risk of heart disease when she is older. Scientists believe that fish contains a fat called omega-3 that protects the heart. In studies of Eskimo Indians, a diet rich in fish appears to be the reason they have fewer heart attacks. Fish rich in these oils include mackerel, herring, tuna, sardines, salmon, and trout. Other kinds of fish carry these oils, too, but in lesser amounts. To get the true health benefits of fish, serve it baked, broiled, or steamed.

Fiber

Fiber is good for the whole family. Studies from the National Cancer Institute show that people who eat a fiber-rich diet of grains and vegetables have a lower cancer risk. A diet richer in fiber may also help keep cholesterol levels in a desirable range by carrying away some of the acids that are needed to make cholesterol. Also, fiber is certainly recognized as an important factor in preventing and treating constipation.

Increase your family's fiber intake by serving the recommended amounts of fruits and vegetables every day. Encourage the use of more whole-grain products, such as cereal and bread. Read product labels to select foods, such as crackers, and snacks with a higher fiber intake. Get your kids in on the decision making, too: have them read and compare labels and sample products that provide more fiber.

FOOD GUIDE PYRAMID: A GUIDE TO DAILY FOOD CHOICES

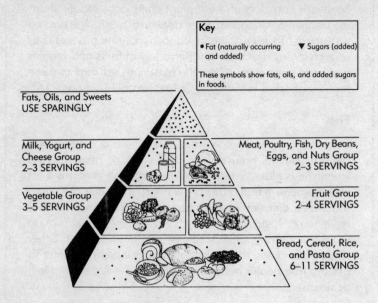

Key
- Fat (naturally occurring and added)   ▼ Sugars (added)

These symbols show fats, oils, and added sugars in foods.

Fats, Oils, and Sweets
USE SPARINGLY

Milk, Yogurt, and Cheese Group
2–3 SERVINGS

Meat, Poultry, Fish, Dry Beans, Eggs, and Nuts Group
2–3 SERVINGS

Vegetable Group
3–5 SERVINGS

Fruit Group
2–4 SERVINGS

Bread, Cereal, Rice, and Pasta Group
6–11 SERVINGS

WHAT COUNTS AS ONE SERVING?

Breads, Cereals, Rice, and Pasta
1 slice of bread
1/2 cup of cooked rice or pasta
1/2 cup of cooked cereal
1 oz. of ready-to-eat cereal

Fruits
1 piece of fruit or melon wedge
3/4 cup of juice
1/2 cup of canned fruit
1/4 cup of dried fruit

Vegetables
1/2 cup of chopped raw or cooked vegetables
1 cup of leafy raw vegetables

Milk, Yogurt, and Cheese
1 cup of milk or yogurt
1 1/2 to 2 oz. of cheese

Fats, Oils, and Sweets
Limit calories from these, especially if you need to lose weight

Meat, Poultry, Fish, Dry Beans, Eggs, and Nuts
2 1/2 to 3 oz. of cooked lean meat, poultry, or fish
Count 1/2 cup of cooked beans or 1 egg or 2 tbsp. of peanut butter as 1 oz. of lean meat (about 1/3 serving)

> **The amount you eat may be more than one serving. For example, a dinner portion of spaghetti would count as two or three servings of pasta.**

Source: *FDA Consumer,* Vol. 26, No. 6, U.S. Department of Health and Human Services, July–August, 1992.

The tip of the pyramid does not count as a major food group. Fats, oils, and sweets provide mostly calories and not much in the way of nutrients. Mostly condiments—not whole foods—are contained here. There is no recommended serving amount; instead, parents are asked to serve these foods sparingly. The words *use sparingly* are likely to have little meaning to your youngster, but perhaps the fat and sugar symbols will. My kids now know that the food groups with the fewer triangular (sugar) and circular (fat) symbols are the food groups Mom likes best. The concentration of symbols in each food group represents the relative amount of fat or sugar that is found in one food group as compared to another food group.

Don't be overzealous about restricting your child's fat intake, either. The American Academy of Pediatrics (AAP) has expressed concerns over emphasizing lower intakes of fat, cholesterol, and salt along with higher intakes of high-fiber cereal, grains, and plant products. A low-fat diet is believed to decrease the risk of heart disease later in life, but a low-fat, plant-based diet could be too low in calories to meet the needs of growing kids. The AAP urges moderation for older children, but infants and toddlers should never be put on low-fat diets. Parents who want to feed a safe, low-fat diet to their children over 2 years of age can do so by following these simple suggestions: serve low-fat dairy products (after age 2), trim meats of visible fat, and bake or broil instead of frying. Make foods from the bread, cereal, rice, and pasta group the foundation of all your meals. Avoid high-fat snack foods that contain more than 5 grams of fat per serving, particularly if they replace more nutritious foods. In addition to promoting healthy eating, parents should encourage regular exercise.

It is impossible to know exactly how much food a young child needs every day. Nutritional needs are determined by growth, activity level, and the type of food being eaten. In our house, I serve at least the minimum suggested servings from each food group. I find that fruits and vegetables are hardest to get my kids to eat, but I serve at least three fruits and two vegetables each day. If they are hungry, they can chose second helpings from any food group they want as long as they have already eaten the basics from every food group.

Snacks are very important to growing kids. Don't be afraid to serve food between meals, but do use the Food Guide Pyramid to make decisions about what you serve. Encourage snacks from the base of the pyramid, since these are the foods we need most. Graham crackers would be a serving from the bread, cereal, rice, and pasta group; a snack of sliced apples can count as a serving of fruit. As long as your child is selecting a variety of foods, he will be well nourished.

☙ THERE IS NO ACCOUNTING FOR TASTE

A child's preference for food will be strongly influenced by the foods served and eaten around her. Though she might initially turn her nose up at some of your favorite meals, over time she will adopt many of the same food likes and dislikes as her parents. Food preference is not an entirely random event. How a food tastes, smells, looks, and even feels in the mouth are all qualities that will determine whether the food will be eaten or refused. All children begin with a preference for sweet tastes and a dislike for bitter or sour tastes. This is a built-in protection against accidental poisonings, since toxic substances are most likely to taste sour or bitter. Infants and children are indifferent to the taste of salt, at least initially, but once it is added to food, it can be a learned and preferred taste.

Mother Nature seems to have endowed the human body with an innate desire to select a variety of food. Studies show that the pleasantness of food declines as it is eaten, and this is not based on satiety. More food is likely to be

FOOD POISONING

Our children, because of their small size and developing immune system, can be seriously harmed by food poisoning. USFDA officials estimate that we experience some form of food-borne illness every 2 years, but we don't identify it as such. Symptoms, which we attribute to the flu, can include nausea, vomiting, diarrhea, fever, and breathing difficulty. Always alert your doctor when you do suspect food poisoning, because in some cases, it can cause death.

So how do you reduce your child's food-poisoning risk? Follow this simple rule: keep hot food hot, cold food cold, and always keep the kitchen clean.

Bacteria causes food poisoning. Cooking kills bacteria, and refrigeration prevents bacteria from growing. At room temperature (anywhere between 60°F and 125°F), bacteria will multiply like crazy. Meat, poultry, fish, and dairy are the foods bacteria like best, but even unwashed fruit and vegetable skins and dishes made with mayonnaise can carry unwanted bacteria.

- Cook all foods to at least 165°F. (Get a small thermometer to take the guesswork out of barbecuing and roasting.) This goes for reheated food, too.
- Keep your refrigerator temperature at 40°F and your freezer at 0°F.
- Keep cold food in the refrigerator until ready to serve, cook, or reheat.
- Thaw frozen food in the refrigerator and then cook it the same day.
- Cook ground beef, turkey, or pork until all the pink is gone.
- When using a microwave oven to cook or reheat, make sure all parts of the meal are equally cooked through.
- To keep school lunches safe, place a small freezer pack in with cold foods.
- Keep eggs in the refrigerator, throw out eggs with a cracked shell, and cook eggs until they aren't runny.

- ▪ If your kids love eating raw cookie dough, use a liquid egg substitute when baking instead of fresh eggs. These products are pasteurized and do not carry the risk of salmonella as do raw, fresh eggs.
- ▪ Keep it clean. Cross-contamination from hands, dirty cutting boards, and countertops is a common way to spread bacteria.
- ▪ Finally, don't rely on your nose to sniff out contaminated food. Some foods can be tainted even if they are not smelly.

consumed when a meal contains several different foods instead of one or two items, increasing the likelihood that your child will eat enough food to satisfy nutrient needs. If you want your child to eat more, you may find success when you offer small servings of several different foods instead of a large serving of just one food.

With all these built in biological and psychological taste and preference controls, you might wonder if you can trust your child's ability to select a healthy diet. Over 60 years ago, researcher Clara Davis first looked at this issue and found that when they are given nutritious choices, children can select a diet that is nutritionally adequate even without adult supervision. In 1991, Leann Birch, Ph.D., took a more contemporary look at the question of a child's ability to self-regulate food intake. Over a 6-day period, Dr. Birch kept track of the food eaten by 15 children ages 2 to 5. If the kids ate a little at one meal, they compensated by eating more at the next, or vice versa. At the end of any given day they had consumed almost exactly the same total amount of calories as the day before or the following day. The study results showed that what children eat at any given meal is likely to be quite variable, but that in the end, it all seems to balance out. For example, one child in the Birch study, offered the same foods at breakfast 2 days in a row, consumed food with only 100 calories one day, but with 350 calories the next. You do not need to coerce your child into eating—you can stop using threats or bribes forever. In fact, results of at least one study done with preschoolers showed that parents who have a very authoritarian and controlling attitude about what their kids eat actually impede their children's ability to learn how to control food. The researchers suggest to parents that it is best to offer a variety of nutritious food and allow the child to select the type and amounts they want to eat.

This does not mean you should be cavalier about what your child eats. In a public health report released in 1994 regarding 1,392 children aged 1 to 10 who participated in a nationwide food consumption survey, it was noted that vitamins A, C, and E, calcium, iron, and zinc were the nutrients most often consumed in amounts below recommended levels. The percentage of calories from fat, saturated fat, and sodium were above levels recommended for most children. This shows that despite the body's innate mechanisms to keep your child on the right nutrition course, she can easily fall off the path.

Our children are exposed to many more kinds of foods than we were as kids. Ready-to-eat snack and convenience foods and low-nutrient drinks have replaced the once-traditional snack foods of juice and crackers or milk and cookies. Much of what children learn about food comes from television; it is important for you to appreciate the impact this medium has on what your child eats. According to a 1985 Nielsen report, children aged 6 to 11 years watch approximately 26 hours of TV per week and see between 30,000 and 40,000 television commercials each year. Advertisers spend $700 million to advertise during children's TV programming. Unfortunately, they are not trying to persuade your child to eat his peas and carrots. More likely, they are promoting cereal that contains 3 to 6 teaspoons of sugar per serving or juice products that carry pictures of fruit but actually contain only 10 to 15 percent real fruit juice. TV is not all bad, but studies clearly show that kids are at greater risk of obesity and are generally less active if they watch a lot of TV.

It is now common for both parents to be working away from home. Working mothers often worry that the meals served in their homes are not as nutritious as in those of mothers who are at home full-time. The 1987–1988 Nationwide Food Consumption Survey also looked at the effect maternal employment had on young children's diets. Although a number of dietary problems—such as a lower than recommended intake of calcium, iron, zinc, and vitamin E—were found, it was not because more mothers were working. This survey's results indicated that working moms are doing just as good a job at feeding their kids as mothers at home but that there is room for improvement all the way around. *Most* households could do better at serving nutritious meals.

✄ FOOD AND ILLNESS

All this useful information about nutrition and food preferences will most likely be set aside when your child becomes ill. One of the first signs of illness is loss of appetite. Fear, stress, and pain can also suppress appetite. A child who fears he may vomit is certainly not going to eat. A shot or a trip to the doctor are events that can create stress and kill your child's appetite. Pain from a sore throat or bad tummy-ache can squelch the desire for food, too.

When illness turns off a usually robust appetite, don't panic. The body is prepared for this emergency. When your child does not eat, her body will automatically turn to the energy it has in reserve in the form of a substance known as glycogen. If glycogen stores have been used up, muscle tissue can be changed to amino acids that can be converted into glucose and used for fuel. If absolutely necessary, the liver can turn stored fat into ketones and use this as fuel, too.

While the body relies on its stored sources of fuel and nutrients, what you can do is offer fluids in the form of ice chips, water, or even fruit juice, if your child will drink it. In some cases of diarrhea or vomiting, the pediatrician may ask you to add a drink like Pedialyte. It contains minerals that may be depleted during prolonged vomiting or diarrhea. You'll read more about the need for fluid under specific problems in chapter 3. What is important for you as the parent to grasp is that good nutrition will count during illness, but it often cannot be fully supplied *during* illness: the time to worry about nutrition is *before* your child becomes ill. The well-nourished child will have a healthy supply of nutrients to draw upon when ill and may even be able to resist and fight off more illness.

❧ PUTTING IT ALL TOGETHER

Food is a great medium through which to express your love and concern for your family. The Norman Rockwell image of one big happy family gathered around the table for a meal might be our ideal, but times have changed, and along with it, the family meal. A relaxed Friday-night family dinner at the local pizza parlor complete with laughs and hot, yummy pizza certainly has a place in family life today. Though a good meal should include lots of vegetables, whole grains, and the like, there is certainly room for all the foods kids love, too, like chocolate-chip cookies and ice cream. Even parents who are very conscientious about their children's diet should experience the pleasure of the occasional break in routine.

The best way to know how well you are doing at providing healthful meals and how well your child is doing at actually eating them is to keep a 24-hour food diary and compare it to the suggested servings on the Food Guide

FOOD DIARY

TIME	FOOD	AMOUNT
Breakfast		
Morning snack		
Lunch		
Afternoon snack		
Dinner		
Evening snack		

Number of Food Group Servings:

Milk/cheese/yogurt: _____

Meat/fish/poultry/beans/nuts/tofu: _____

Fruit: _____

Vegetables: _____

Bread/cereal/rice/pasta: _____

Pyramid on page 16. Remember to include the foods eaten at the day-care center, school, or at parties. Include beverages, too. It is the rare child (or even adult) who eats exactly as recommended, but the food diary can plainly point out just how well your child is doing at getting the foods—from all the food groups—that she needs. It will also help you keep track of the amount of foods consumed in the less nutritious fats, oils, and sweets group. Though you might think your efforts at healthy eating often go unappreciated by your child or are even looked upon with disdain when you serve fruit instead of candy as snacks, the type and quality of food you serve your child can have a profound effect on his health for all his life.

➤ MAKING IT LOOK GOOD

Special foods make a child feel cared for, and so can decorations and fancy utensils. We have a set of sturdy, inexpensive cut-glass goblets out of which my kids love to eat pudding and ice cream when they're sick. Of course, straws are always popular, and so is being allowed to eat on the couch or in bed—just select food items that are not likely to be too messy or spill too easily. A lap tray, available at many stores that sell household goods, can be a good investment. It will be used many times over the years.

Try some of these decorative suggestions:

- Serve a pear half with a face made of raisins and with carrot-curl hair.
- Serve pudding or ice cream in an ice cream cone.
- Use candy canes as swizzle sticks in warm tea or milk shakes.
- Serve food on fancy plates or even birthday- or party-type paper plates.
- Put flowers on the food tray.
- Use pretty place mats and napkins.

✍ VITAMIN AND MINERAL SUPPLEMENTS

The official position from the AAP and other medical organizations is that healthy kids don't need vitamin and mineral supplements. A well-balanced diet is recommended as the source of all nutrients. The only exception to this is if a child is anorexic, eats a very poor diet, or is on such a restrictive diet for obesity that nutrient intake is likely to be low. Children with chronic diseases, such as cystic fibrosis or inflammatory bowel disease (IBD), may need a supplement. In limited cases, specific nutrients are recommended—for example, vitamin B_{12} for children eating very strict vegetarian diets, iron for the treatment of iron-deficiency anemia, and fluoride if there is insufficient fluoride in the local water supply.

Though health survey results do not find full-fledged nutrient deficiencies in healthy kids, parents still worry about their children's diet and often give vitamins "just for insurance." Recognizing that parents are likely to turn to multivitamins, the Food and Drug Administration (FDA) regulates the nutrient content of supplements marketed to children. Children's multivitamins must keep nutrients in a range of 25 to 150 percent of the recommended dietary allowances for any given nutrient. This means that you can give your child a children's multivitamin mineral supplement in the directed amounts without fear of giving him a dose too large for his small body.

Single-nutrient supplements are not recommended for children except in the specific situations mentioned above. Excessive doses of some nutrients can be harmful: vitamins A and D can be toxic; niacin can cause flushing and irregular heartbeat; vitamin B_6 can cause numbness and neurological disorders. You must be alert to the danger of accidental poisoning from supplements because to kids, vitamins look like candy and must be kept out of reach, just like any medicine.

THE NUTRITION FACTS PANEL

You'll see the nutrition facts panel on almost every food. Use it to evaluate nutrition claims and to choose lower fat snacks and convenience foods. Baby foods do not carry information about fat and calories from fat, cholesterol, or saturated fat because there is no need to limit fat in children under age 2.

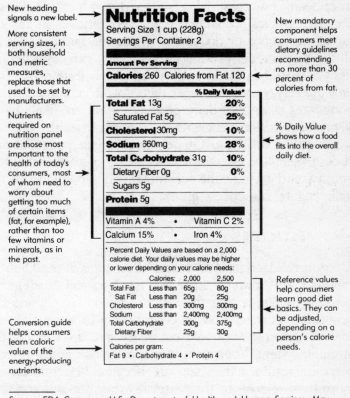

New heading signals a new label. →

More consistent serving sizes, in both household and metric measures, replace those that used to be set by manufacturers.

Nutrients required on nutrition panel are those most important to the health of today's consumers, most of whom need to worry about getting too much of certain items (fat, for example), rather than too few vitamins or minerals, as in the past.

Conversion guide helps consumers learn caloric value of the energy-producing nutrients.

New mandatory component helps consumers meet dietary guidelines recommending no more than 30 percent of calories from fat.

% Daily Value shows how a food fits into the overall daily diet.

Reference values help consumers learn good diet basics. They can be adjusted, depending on a person's calorie needs.

Nutrition Facts

Serving Size 1 cup (228g)
Servings Per Container 2

Amount Per Serving

Calories 260 Calories from Fat 120

% Daily Value*

Total Fat 13g	**20**%
Saturated Fat 5g	**25**%
Cholesterol 30mg	**10**%
Sodium 360mg	**28**%
Total Carbohydrate 31g	**10**%
Dietary Fiber 0g	**0**%
Sugars 5g	
Protein 5g	

Vitamin A 4%	•	Vitamin C 2%
Calcium 15%	•	Iron 4%

* Percent Daily Values are based on a 2,000 calorie diet. Your daily values may be higher or lower depending on your calorie needs:

	Calories:	2,000	2,500
Total Fat	Less than	65g	80g
Sat Fat	Less than	20g	25g
Cholesterol	Less than	300mg	300mg
Sodium	Less than	2,400mg	2,400mg
Total Carbohydrate		300g	375g
Dietary Fiber		25g	30g

Calories per gram:
Fat 9 • Carbohydrate 4 • Protein 4

Source: *FDA Consumer,* U.S. Department of Health and Human Services, May, 1993.

➤ VEGETARIAN EATING

Some 12 million Americans now say that they eat a vegetarian diet, which means that a lot more kids than ever before are eating that way, too. A vegetarian diet can be adequate in all nutrients, including protein and iron. Surprisingly, vegetarians do not have a greater risk of iron-deficiency anemia even though red meat is one of the best sources of this mineral. Children who are not meat eaters get their iron from beans, potatoes, dried fruit, and iron-fortified cereals, and their bodies probably become very efficient at absorbing all the iron they do ingest. Vegetarian families that include dairy and egg products in their diets can easily get the right balance of protein and the essential vitamin B_{12}. It is only the very, very strict vegan diets—which eliminate meat, poultry, eggs, and all dairy products—that are likely to be at risk of nutrition deficiencies. To select a healthy vegetarian diet, use the Food Guide Pyramid (see page 16) and choose beans or eggs instead of beef, or tofu instead of poultry, and include the recommended servings from the milk, yogurt, and cheese group.

➤ PESTICIDES

A report released in 1993 called "Pesticides in the Diets of Infants and Children," issued by the National Academy of Sciences, suggests that the American food supply and the pesticides it carries may be contributing to serious illness, such as cancer, nervous-system injury, and disorders of the immune system. Your child is at greater risk of harm from pesticide residues than you are because (1) children eat more food relative to their size, (2) they are still growing, and (3) they will have a higher lifetime exposure than you because more pesticides are used now than when you were a child. The best strategy for parents is to minimize a child's intake of pesticides. This is no easy task, given that pesticide residues are invisible. Here are some practical tips you can try:

- Wash all produce.
- Use a scrub brush on all foods with edible skins, such as carrots and potatoes.
- Peel waxed fruits and vegetables, such as cucumbers and apples. Wax, used to make the food look appealing, can seal in pesticides.
- Discard the outside leaves of lettuce, kale, and cabbage.
- Buy domestic produce. Pesticides on imported produce may carry illegal pesticide residues. Ask your produce market to label the origin of the food.
- Trim fats from meats; do not eat poultry skin. Pesticides are often carried in the fatty part of foods.
- Fish and seafood products contain pesticide residues. Cod, pollock, haddock, and canned tuna are better choices.
- Serve low-fat dairy products after your child is 2 years old. (If your child is having trouble gaining weight, ask the child's doctor about the use of low-fat dairy products.)
- Buy certified organic foods when possible. These foods often look imperfect, but they taste good. They often cost more than nonorganic foods, but purchasing them sends a message to farmers that there is a market for organic produce.
- Shop at farmers' markets when they're open for the season. Locally grown and sold foods may not carry the preservatives that are required when foods are shipped.
- Vary your child's diet as much as possible. This way, if it turns out that a particular food carries pesticides, at least you won't have been serving tons of it for years.

~2~

BEING PREPARED

Do you remember the first time you had to take your child's temperature? I do. It was early evening on a holiday weekend. I had a houseful of relatives and my daughter was crying and felt warm. David and I decided we had better check her temperature. We had a rectal thermometer, given to us courtesy of our hospital, but we had no idea how to use it safely. She squirmed, fussed, and cried even louder at our clumsy efforts. We eventually abandoned our goal for fear we would do more harm than good.

Fortunately, Sarah didn't get any worse. The incident made it clear to me that here was another area in which a child had changed our family needs. Before we had any children, a bottle of aspirin and a box of adhesive bandages was all we kept in our medicine cabinet. If we needed cough drops or cold medicine, we went out and bought it then. With children, that changes. Parents who have to dress a sick child in order to get a required medicine are likely to feel a bit annoyed with themselves since planning could have eliminated the need for the trip and kept the child in his warm, comfortable bed. Given that the average preschooler gets about six colds per year and that kids in general seem to get a generous share of cuts and bruises, it is absolutely safe to assume your family will benefit by practical planning. After our thermometer incident, I went out and purchased a digital thermometer and a heat-sensitive thermometer strip, and at Sarah's 4-month checkup, I asked her pediatrician to put in writing the type and amounts of nonprescription medications to stock in our new expanded medicine cabinet. Fearing that injury is as likely to effect my children as illness, I put together a medical kit for the home and car. Use the information in this chapter to prepare for the inevitable sick days and to prevent avoidable accidents.

WHEN TO CALL THE DOCTOR

First things first: not all ailments can be treated at home; some require a pediatrician's opinion. If your child looks unusual or acts oddly, trust your instincts and call the doctor. If your child has projectile vomiting, abdominal pain, or blood in her vomit or stool, get medical advice. In all instances, an infant with diarrhea, fever, vomiting, or breathing difficulties should be seen by a doctor. You may fear waking your pediatrician at night for unnecessary concerns; discuss night calls with your pediatrician ahead of time. You are likely to hear her say that when on call, she expects to be called. Another great late-night resource are the nurses on the maternity ward at the hospital. Someone is always awake and on duty at the hospital.

To make your conversation efficient and useful, be prepared to answer the following questions:

■ What are the symptoms?
■ How long have the symptoms been going on?
■ How old is the child?
■ Does the child act very sick?
■ Has anyone else in the house been ill?
■ Does your child have an underlying condition, such as a chronic disease?

THE FAMILY MEDICAL KIT

Pediatricians and family physicians will often suggest home treatment for minor childhood ailments. If you stock your medicine chest with the supplies suggested below, you will be ready to comply with most any recommended therapy the doctor might suggest.

It's also a very good idea to keep a medical kit in the car. Include all of the starred (*) items below and consider adding a few extras such as a flashlight, bug spray, sunscreen and safety pins.

When you have a baby sitter watching your child, be sure he or she is aware of where you keep your medical kit.

- Adhesive bandages*
  (small and big)
- Aspirin substitute*
  (acetaminophen)
- Antihistamine
- Gauze bandages
- Calamine lotion
- Sterile cotton balls or roll
- Adhesive tape
- Elastic bandages
- Rounded-end tweezers*
- Snub-nosed scissors
- Antiseptic cream*
- Antiseptic wipes*
- Hydrogen peroxide

- Rubbing alcohol
- Syrup of ipecac*
- Hydrocortizone cream
- Oral thermometer
- Rectal thermometer
- Hot-water bottle (I prefer these over heating pads. Do not put them directly on the skin; wrap them in a baby blanket or dish towel to prevent burns.)
- Cold-water bottle
- Eye cup
- Rubber suction bulb

*Approved first-aid manual, such as *The Red Cross Manual*

If the doctor wants to see your child, follow her advice regarding comfort measures. If you must go to the emergency room and the event is not life threatening, *calm down!* This will help your child relax, too. If you are making an emergency visit to the hospital without your pediatrician's knowledge, try to call her—if time permits. Be your child's advocate at the hospital. Tell the staff about his fears, pain, and what you think he might need. If appropriate, ask to talk privately with the doctor. If your child is not being seen by his regular doctor, ask the physician how many children he has seen with this condition. What are the treatment options? What are the treatment risks? How long will the treatment last, and what can your child expect from treatment? Ask that all instructions be written down, particularly if you are by yourself. After the emergency-room visit, inform your pediatrician about the event. The emergency room will send a summation of the visit to your child's doctor, but this will take a few days.

✎ OVER-THE-COUNTER MEDICINES

Ask your doctor about the type of over-the-counter (OTC) medicines she recommends for your child. They include pain reliever, fever reducers, cough and cold medicines.

Aspirin—even those brands developed for children—is no longer recommended because its use has been linked with the development of Reye syndrome, a disease of the liver and brain that can be fatal. Acetaminophen is now the pain reliever and fever buster recommended by pediatricians. It is as effective as aspirin and should be kept in most households. Do be careful with doses. The dose by age, particularly with the liquid formulas, can vary with the manufacturer, so read labels. Recently, acetaminophen use has been linked with liver and kidney failure in adults. The problem occurs in long-term users who consume several alcoholic drinks per day. There has been no link in children

BLOWING THE PAIN AWAY

Researchers at the Children's Hospital in Columbus, Ohio, have come up with an effective way to make immunization shots more bearable. A group of 149 4- to 7-year-old children were taught to blow out air repeatedly, as if they were blowing away bubbles. This blowing technique was used during the administration of routine immunizations and was found to be a simple, quick pain reliever. The blowing offers distraction from painful and stressful shots, in much the same way as the breathing techniques learned by women in childbirth preparation classes. Help your child practice imaginary bubble blowing before her next shot, then see if the technique makes this potentially stressful procedure more tolerable for her.

between acetaminophen and these potentially life-threatening conditions; acetaminophen remains the preferred pain reliever for children. Nevertheless, call the pediatrician if acetaminophen is needed to relieve pain or fever for more than 3 days.

Next to acetaminophen, cold medicines are likely to be the most common OTC medicines families buy. The ingredients and purpose of these preparations vary widely. Do not give a child under 3 years of age cold or cough medicines unless advised by your child's doctor. Expectorants commonly contain guaifenesin, which thins secretions so that they can be coughed up more easily. Decongestants decrease mucus production; their most common ingredients include phenylephrine and pseudoephedrine. These should not be used for more than a few days, and they often cause sleepiness and irritability. Chlorpheniramine and brompheniramine are the ingredients widely used in antihistamines. These medications decrease swelling of the mu-

cous membranes, reducing secretions caused by allergy.
Cough suppressants inhibit the cough reflex.

None of these medications cures the underlying illness.
They can relieve symptoms, allowing a child to get needed
rest, but they should be used judiciously. Symptoms such as
a runny nose and cough are annoying, but they are the
body's attempt to clear secretions and should not automatically be suppressed. Discuss the use of all OTC medications
with your own pediatrician and ask which brands and formulas he recommends.

ANTIBIOTICS

The prescription medicines you are most likely to encounter
are antibiotics. These are medicines that kill or reduce the
bacteria that create infection. They do not kill viruses and
they will not make cold or flu symptoms go away. They are
effective against bacterial infections, such as those that
cause earaches and strep throat. Usually, they are prescribed for 10 days. You can expect your child to feel better
2 to 3 days after starting the medication, but it is important
that she finish *all* the medication—unless otherwise directed—because feeling a bit better does not mean the infection is completely gone.

There is another reason to have your child finish all the
medication. With the increased use of antibiotic therapy in
both children and adults, there is a growing concern about
the number of bacteria resistant to antibiotics. Antibiotics
are effective in fighting illness because they destroy bacteria
or reduce their numbers. Bacteria can become resistant to
antibiotics by developing new ways to replicate or by secret-
ing enzymes that make the antibiotic medication ineffective. You can help prevent antibiotic resistance by having
your child complete the recommended antibiotic dosage. If
an antibiotic is not taken regularly, the antibiotic-resistant
bacteria is able to multiply and prolong the illness. Failure

to take the full recommended course of medication increases the likelihood that the bacteria will recur in a resistant form. The USFDA is tracking bacterial resistance in hopes of understanding the problem and establishing ways to prevent its escalation. New guidelines for treating fluid in the ear may have more doctors taking a "wait and see" approach before turning to antibiotics.

The effect antibiotic therapy can have on nutrition is a concern, particularly when antibiotic therapy must be repeated. Antibiotics can decrease the absorption of essential nutrients such as amino acids, folic acid, vitamin B_{12}, the fat-soluble vitamins (A, D, E and K), calcium, iron, potassium, magnesium, and zinc, but full-fledged nutrition deficiencies caused by antibiotic therapy are not a likely side effect. Vitamin K deficiency can occur when long-term use of antibiotics kills the "friendly" intestinal bacteria that make vitamin K. Cases of vitamin K deficiency have been reported, but only in connection with underlying disease, such as liver disease, or when other medications that suppress vitamin K are taken, too. Children need about 15 to 20 micrograms of vitamin K per day. Even if the intestinal bacteria were ineffective at making vitamin K, the vitamin could be obtained from food: liver, milk, meat, eggs, cereal, fruits, and vegetables are sources of vitamin K. A half cup of broccoli carries over 100 micrograms; a red tomato, 20 micrograms; and even one slice of bread contains about 10 micrograms. The availability of vitamin K from food sources makes a deficiency unlikely.

Antibiotics may destroy the bacteria that keep the yeast *Candida* in control. An overgrowth of *Candida* can cause thrush in the mouth, bowel, diaper area, or vagina that then needs to be treated with an antifungal drug. This is not a common side effect of antibiotic therapy in kids, but if you have concerns about it, discuss it with your pediatrician. Another potentially serious but rare problem that can occur with any antibiotic is pseudomembranous colitis. In this sit-

THE WELL-STOCKED PANTRY

Keep your pantry as well prepared for sick days as you do your medicine cabinet. It is just as difficult to take a sick child to the grocery store as it is to the pharmacy. If you keep a supply of the food items listed below, you will be ready to cook the dishes appropriate for most childhood ailments. I would like to see my kids eating only homemade foods, but to be honest, I must say that when they are sick, they love things like packaged gelatin or canned cream of tomato soup, and sometimes there just isn't enough time to use my homemade pudding recipe. So I make some temporary compromises and include some of these convenience foods, and everyone is happy.

- Gelatin (in a variety of flavors)
- Cans of juice (at least one of them apple)
- Instant pudding
- Canned milk
- Clear soft drinks
- Ice cream
- Sherbet
- Applesauce

- Canned soup
- Rice
- Noodles
- Saltine-type crackers
- Arrowroot cookies
- Cough drops (to prevent choking, smash these into slivers before serving them)

HAND WASHING

If you want to start a habit that will truly reduce the spread of germs in your house, become a hand-washing zealot. Hand washing can prevent the spread of colds and more serious diseases, such as hepatitis. When to wash:

▪ Before eating. Remind your kids to wash their hands before lunch at school.
▪ Before cooking
▪ After handling raw meat
▪ After using the toilet, sneezing, coughing, diaper changing, and handling a pet.

uation, bacteria that are resistant to the bacteria already present multiply in the digestive tract, causing violent, bloody diarrhea. The antibiotic is immediately stopped.

The most common side effects your child is likely to face when on antibiotic therapy are nausea, vomiting, and diarrhea. To reduce the risk of these side effects, follow the food and drink advice on the medication bottle's label. Some antibiotics work best when taken with food; others must be taken with lots of fluids to keep kidneys healthy. Here are some general guidelines:

▪ The penicillin class of antibiotics, which includes amoxicillin and ampicillin, among others, can occasionally cause nausea, vomiting, thirst, and diarrhea. Ampicillin should be taken on an empty stomach.
▪ The cephalosporine antibiotics, which include cefaclor— also known as Ceclor—should be taken on an empty stomach, because food slows down the body's ability to absorb the drug. Diarrhea is common with this class of antibiotic.

- The sulfuramide antibiotics, which include Septra and Gantrisin, should be taken with plenty of fluids. Adequate liquids prevent the formation of potentially damaging crystals in the urine.
- The antibiotic known as erythromycin can cause nausea, vomiting, and diarrhea. When it is taken with meals, the presence of food can prevent these complications.

✎ CHOKING

More than 300 children die each year in America from choking. Food is usually the cause. Careful supervision and thoughtful selection of foods can reduce the risk for your child. The AAP identifies the following items as common choking dangers and offers practical strategies to prevent choking.

Dangerous foods include the following:

- Hot dogs
- Nuts
- Chunks of meat
- Grapes
- Hard candy
- Popcorn
- Chunks of peanut butter
- Raisins
- Raw carrots

Dangerous household items include the following:

- Balloons
- Coins
- Marbles
- Small toy parts
- Pen caps
- Small button–type batteries

Preventive measures are as follows:

- Keep the above foods from your child until she is 4 years of age.
- Insist that your child eat while sitting at the table. She should never walk, run, or play with food in her mouth.
- Prepare and cut food for your young child and teach him to chew his food well.
- Supervise mealtime for your young child. Many choking cases occur when older brothers or sisters offer unsafe foods to a younger child.
- Avoid toys with small parts and keep other small household items out of reach of your young child.

3

ILLNESS AND THE FOOD CONNECTION

The food recommendations included in this chapter are based on sound nutrition principles. For example, when your child has a fever, his need for energy and fluid increases, making high-calorie liquids a good food choice. If your child has iron-deficiency anemia, she needs to eat foods rich in absorbable iron. If your little boy is wetting the bed, constipation could be a complicating problem, and more fiber might be the cure. If a trip to the dentist reveals cavities, a change from starchy snacks to ones with more protein could be the answer. Of course, food cannot replace medical treatment, and all food remedies are not benign. Too much cod liver oil, for example, can lead to excessive build-up in the body of vitamins A and D. Even some herbal teas have been known to contain toxic ingredients capable of causing organ damage. Follow the advice of your doctor regarding medication and pain relievers, and then follow the food recommendations here that apply to your child's condition.

Always call your pediatrician first when your child is sick. Use this chapter *after* your doctor has diagnosed the problem and you are seeking detailed advice about how to feed and comfort your child. The information that follows is meant to supplement the advice you receive from your medical practitioner.

⤇ ASTHMA

Asthma is a chronic lung condition. Eight to 13 percent of U.S. children have asthma, and the numbers seem to be climbing, particularly for kids under 17 years old who live in the city. It often develops around age 4 to 5 and is more likely to occur in boys than girls, perhaps because boys have smaller airways. During an asthma attack, breathing tubes are blocked either by mucus, muscle spasm, or swelling, and symptoms such as wheezing, difficulty in breathing, and coughing occur.

Sensitivity to animal dander, pollen, dust, mold, some foods, and food additives can trigger an asthma attack. Keep in mind that excessive exercise, particularly in cold weather, or a routine cold can also cause asthma symptoms. In some infants, gastroesophageal reflux (GER), a condition in which a small amount of the stomach contents is regurgitated up into the throat, affects the breathing tubes and becomes a cause of wheezing.

During an asthma attack, it is essential to stop the bronchospasm and restore normal breathing. The doctor may advise administering such drugs as antihistamines, bronchodilators, or steroids. An individual treatment plan for each child must be developed, with the doctor, child, and family acting as a team.

The good news about asthma is that most kids outgrow it; the prognosis for childhood asthma is excellent. In a study of 2,345 British children who had at least one wheezing episode before their fifth birthday, 80 percent of these kids were free of wheezing by their tenth birthday. Though symptoms can reappear, most kids are virtually free of breathing difficulties except during an upper respiratory infection or vigorous exercise.

ASTHMA AND THE FOOD CONNECTION: PREVENTING TRIGGER ILLNESSES

Public health studies have found many children eat diets low in vitamins A, C, and E. These nutrients are essential to a healthy immune system and proper growth. By ensuring that your child has adequate nutrition, you may help your child resist upper respiratory infections that can bring on an asthma attack:

- Serve at least one vitamin C–rich food daily, such as orange juice, strawberries, oranges, kiwi, or other vitamin C–fortified juices.
- Offer a variety of vegetables. These contain vitamins, minerals, and substances known as phytochemicals that may help resist infection by keeping the immune system strong.
- If your child is a picky eater, use a children's multivitamin and mineral supplement. Read about their proper use on page 26.

SALT AND ASTHMA

Evidence of a link between salt and asthma is emerging. In a study of 22 men with mild to moderate asthma, it was found that the men had fewer symptoms (such as wheezing) and used a bronchodilator less often while on a low-sodium diet than did those on a high-sodium diet. The improvement shown in the study was only a modest one, but a lower salt diet is a worthwhile goal for most families. Most kids eat more salt than they need:

- When your infant starts on table food, don't automatically salt it.
- Keep the salt shaker off the table.
- Frequently serve fresh fruits and vegetables as snacks instead of salted snack foods.

FOOD ALLERGIES

Food allergies are rarely the main aggravating factor in the development of asthma, but there is a clear link between the two. In a study of 140 children thought to have a food allergy, 6 percent developed wheezing when challenged with an allergenic food. In another study of 25 patients with food allergy, a food challenge provoked a wheezing attack, accompanied by eczema and skin rashes, in 20 percent of the participants. To reduce the risk of a food allergy–induced asthma attack in your child:

▪ Keep a food diary to identify food allergies.
▪ Pay attention to your child's skin. Rashes often accompany a food allergy–induced asthma attack.
▪ Fish, nuts, peanuts, eggs, and milk are the most common allergenic foods; do not serve them until your baby is at least 10 months of age.
▪ Breast-feed your child. Breast-feeding will not guarantee your child will be allergy free, but it is likely to reduce the risk of allergies or at least postpone their onset.
▪ Delay introducing solid foods until the appropriate time to reduce the risk of food allergy.
▪ Contact:
Mothers of Asthmatics
Food Allergy Information Resources
10875 Main Street
Suite 210
Fairfax, VA 22030
(703) 385-4403

SULFITE SENSITIVITY

Asthma is the most common and severe adverse reaction attributed to sulfite ingestion. Sulfites have been used in wine and as a food additive to keep cut fruits and vegetables looking fresh and to prevent spoiling in shrimp. The number of asthmatics who are sulfite sensitive varies from 1 percent to as high as 10 percent. Asthmatics who are sulfite sensitive have difficulty breathing within minutes of sulfite ingestion, and sulfite-induced asthma attacks have resulted in death. It is speculated that some people are sulfite sensitive because their bodies lack the ability to change sulfite into sulfate, its harmless form. Because sulfites have the ability to trigger severe reactions, the use of sulfite was banned in 1985, but the ban does not cover fresh-cut potatoes, dried fruit, or wine, and sulfites are still present in many foods (see list below). If your child is asthmatic, consider whether attacks may be related to sulfite ingestion. If you suspect sulfite sensitivity, observe your child and keep a food intake record. Also do the following:

▪ If your child is sulfite sensitive, avoid all sulfite-containing foods and medication.
▪ Alert teachers, day-care providers, and home-room parents about this problem.
▪ Educate your child about potential sources of sulfites.
▪ Before administering any medication, consult with your pharmacist regarding the product's sulfite content.

When foods contain sulfite residues that exceed 10 parts per million (ppm), it is required by law that the food label indicate this. Foods with less than 10 ppm are not so labeled and are not associated with sulfite-induced reactions. Foods likely to have a high sulfite content include:

▪ Dried fruit (excluding dark raisins and prunes)
▪ Lime juice (nonfrozen)
▪ Molasses
▪ Grape juice (white, white sparkling, pink sparkling, red sparkling)
▪ Lemon juice (nonfrozen)
▪ Wine
▪ Sauerkraut juice

Foods likely to have a moderate sulfite content include:

- Dried potatoes
- Gravies, sauces
- Maraschino cherries
- Shrimp (fresh)
- Pickled peppers
- Pickles/relishes
- Wine vinegar
- Fruit topping
- Pectin
- Sauerkraut
- Pickled cocktail onions

Foods likely to have a low sulfite content (foods with a low content have not been found to induce reactions) include:

- Hominy
- Maple syrup
- Jams and jellies
- Malt vinegar
- Canned potatoes
- Soft drinks
- Pizza dough (frozen)
- Sugar (especially beet sugar)
- Coconut
- Crackers
- High-fructose corn syrup
- Frozen potatoes
- Beer
- Fresh mushrooms
- Dried cod
- Dry soup mix
- Instant tea
- Pie dough

- Gelatin
- Fresh fruit salad
- Cookies
- Grapes

GASTROESOPHAGEAL REFLUX IN INFANTS

If your pediatrician has identified GER as a condition that aggravates your child's asthma, she may suggest the following techniques to alleviate the problem:

- Serve thickened foods—if your child is eating solids.
- Try not to overfeed; ask your doctor about smaller, more frequent meals.
- After feeding your infant, keep him in a prone position and elevate the head of the bed. This will allow gravity to help keep food in your baby's tummy.

CHILI PEPPERS

Chili peppers irritate the nose and throat, causing the secretion of small amounts of fluid that may make coughing and sneezing easier. It is capsaicin—the compound that gives chilies their fiery taste—that carries this medicinal effect. Most kids cannot tolerate hot chilies; the peppers can also cause skin and mouth irritations. If your child likes mild chilies in the form of salsa, offer it to her. Not only will it contain some of the capsaicin, but it is a flavorful alternative to salt and a good source of vitamin C.

CAFFEINE

Caffeine is very similar to the prescription asthma drug theophylline; for this reason, it may give relief to asthmatics by opening up their airways. Caffeine for the treatment of asthma has no practical application. In an emergency—

when there are no alternatives—caffeine from cola, coffee, or chocolate might be of use. However, caffeine also acts as a stimulant, which has no place in a child's diet in large amounts on a regular basis.

APPROXIMATE CAFFEINE CONTENT OF FOODS AND BEVERAGES

FOOD OR BEVERAGE	CAFFEINE CONTENT (mg)
12 oz. cola	37
6 oz. coffee	103
6 oz. brewed tea	36
1 oz. chocolate candy	13
1 chocolate fudge pop	3
1/2 cup chocolate pudding	4
8 oz. chocolate milk	8
6 oz. hot chocolate from mix	4
2 tbsp. chocolate syrup	5
1 slice chocolate cake with chocolate frosting	10

FISH OILS

Fish and the oils they contain have been helpful in relieving lung inflammation. Results of a recent Australian study of 500 asthmatic children showed that children who ate oily fish more than once a week had half the rate of asthma as kids who did not eat fish. Salmon, herring, and fresh tuna were most effective; canned tuna was not effective. Serve fish to your child when he is young and he is likely to develop a taste for it that will last a lifetime. Certainly offer the oily fish recommended in the Australian study, but don't forget about other fish. Kids particularly like fish steaks and fish fillets. Canned tuna fish is still a good food, and, of course, fish sticks are a favorite of kids, though processing removes some of the healthy benefits and adds some extra fat. Here is some advice regarding fish in your child's diet:

- Fish is a food often suspected of causing allergies in young children. Do not serve it before your child is 10 months old. Be alert to allergy symptoms.
- Serve fish once or twice a week. Try to make one of these choices fresh tuna, salmon, or herring.
- Do not give your child fish-oil capsules or cod liver oil. Fish-oil capsules have not been tested on children, and prolonged use of cod liver oil could result in excessive intake of vitamins A and D.

ASTHMA MEDICATIONS

If your child must take asthma medication, you should note the following:

- Some asthma medications may effect growth rate. Monitor your child's weight. Ask your pediatrician for reasonable weight ranges for height and age.
- If a medication such as Aerobid causes hoarseness or dry mouth, ask your child to rinse with water or a mouthwash after use and encourage her to drink fluids throughout the day.
- Alert the doctor if diarrhea, nausea, or stomach-aches accompany the use of medication. Such side effects might be the result of a slight overdose. A review of dose might eliminate the side effects and make eating more pleasant.
- The medication Theo-Dur, or theophylline, is a chemical cousin of caffeine. Do not allow your child to consume large amounts of caffeine-containing beverages if she is taking this medication.
- Discuss with the pharmacist whether asthma medication is to be taken with food.

HOME COMFORT AND MANAGEMENT TIPS

To help prevent or lessen the impact of asthma attacks, you can take the following steps:

- Develop a crisis plan. The longer an acute asthma attack lasts, the worse it can become.
- Identify food or environmental triggers.
- Avoid smoke, paint fumes, perfumes, and aerosol sprays.
- Minimize cooking fumes; have a good kitchen fan.
- If your kitchen is not well ventilated, use an outside barbecue grill instead of an inside broiler.
- Control environmental allergens such as dust and pet dander.
- Contact the organization Mothers of Asthmatics (see address on page 44).
- Ask your doctor about proper breathing techniques.
- If stress is a trigger, teach your child the relaxation techniques described in Chapter 5 on pages 266–68.
- Do your best to minimize your child's exposure to cold viruses.
- Control exertion, but don't eliminate exercise entirely. Even some Olympic athletes have asthma.
- Use caution in very cold air, high winds, or quick changes in temperature.

RECIPES

SOUTH-OF-THE-BORDER SALSA

YIELD: 1½ CUPS

When your little one reaches for the salt shaker to flavor his burger or season a vegetable, ask him to try this salt-free topping instead. It's a great source of vitamin C and an easy way to increase your child's vegetable intake. It's also great as a snack with toasted tortillas or bagel chips.

2 large ripe tomatoes
1 small onion, minced
1 tsp. chili powder
4-oz. can mild green chilis, rinsed and chopped
1 tsp. lemon juice
2 tbsp. chopped fresh parsley or coriander

1. To remove the skins from the tomatoes: plunge the whole tomatoes into a pot of boiling water for 2 minutes, then into a pot of cold water for 2 minutes. Now the skins can easily be peeled off. Chop the tomatoes into bite-sized chunks.
2. In a glass bowl, combine all remaining ingredients. The salsa can be served right away but will taste even better in an hour or so. Keep refrigerated.

SIMPLE SALMON

YIELD: 2 SERVINGS

Most kids love this pretty pink fish as long as it is not over-cooked.. Count on your microwave to prepare salmon perfectly.

> **8 oz. fresh salmon steaks, cut into 2-in. cubes**
> **1 tsp. Italian salad dressing**

1. Arrange the chunks of fish in a circle on a glass pie plate. Brush with the Italian dressing.
2. Cover and cook on high for 3 minutes. Let rest for another 3 minutes to complete cooking. All microwave ovens cook differently, so make sure that the fish is firm when pressed with a finger and that it is pale pink, with no deep-rose spots. Cook 1 additional minute if it is not cooked through.

OVEN FISH FRY

YIELD: 2 OR 3 PORTIONS

Of all the ways to prepare fish, kids often like the crispy texture of fried fish best, but the extra fat from frying is not very healthful. My kids love this as a main dish or served in a fresh bun as a sandwich. It even tastes good topped with South-of-the-Border Salsa (see recipe on page 51).

> **8-oz. fish fillet (haddock, halibut, and sole are good choices)**
> **1 large egg, beaten**
> **¹/₂ to 1 cup seasoned bread crumbs**

1. Preheat oven to 375°F. Cut the fillet into 2 or 3 pieces. Dip the fish into the egg, then roll it in the bread crumbs.
2. Cook the fillet on a lightly oiled baking sheet for 20 minutes. Turn it after 10 minutes of cooking so both sides crisp evenly.

✕ BED WETTING (ENURESIS)

Bed wetting is a common problem and potentially a great source of family stress. At age 5, 92 percent of children are dry during the day, but only 80 percent of these kids are dry at night. It is not until age 12 that 95 percent of children are dry at night. Children are likely to have a wet bed for several reasons. Many kids are deep sleepers, too sleepy to wake up even when their bladders are full. Children also have smaller bladders than adults. Some researchers believe that the problem may be caused by hormones: at night, secretions of vasopressin, the antidiuretic hormone, may decrease, resulting in poor bladder control and ultimately bed wetting. There is also a strong familial incidence. If one parent in a family was a bed wetter, then the children each have a 40 percent chance of being one, too, and if both parents were bed wetters, the chance jumps to 70 percent for each child.

Not all causes of bed wetting are benign. Occasionally, the cause can be a structural problem or a urinary tract infection. Diabetes mellitus or neurological abnormalities can also be medical reasons for the problem. Constipation, which is common in children, can make the problem worse by decreasing the functional capacity of the bladder. Disease and structural or neurological problems are uncommon causes of enuresis, but it is important that a physician rule them out. In some cases, the doctor might prescribe medication to decrease the frequency of urination, but such medications are generally used for a very specific and short length of time because of potential side effects. In most cases, the best medicine the pediatrician will provide is reassurance. In the absence of a physical or medical cause, time and physical maturity are looked to as the cures. In most cases, bed wetting corrects itself spontaneously.

BED WETTING AND THE FOOD CONNECTION

Since the need to urinate is directly related to the amounts of fluid ingested, taking a thoughtful look at what your child is eating and drinking before bed is advised. Remember that solids like ice cream, gelatin, yogurt, and pudding all become liquid when swallowed and digested. Juicy fruits like oranges, watermelon, or grapes contain their own source of natural fluid. Juice, particularly that sold in juice boxes marketed toward kids, can result in a high fluid intake. Because boxed juices are sweet and have appealing packages, some kids can easily consume one or two of these without really thinking about it. Caffeine is a diuretic, meaning it makes the body urinate more. If your child is getting a dose of caffeine in the form of chocolate candy, hot chocolate, or iced tea before bed, it might be adding to the problem. To help cut down on bed wetting:

■ Do not restrict fluids, but do observe what your child eats and drinks before bed and see if a connection can be made.
■ Instead of serving juice, milk, or soda (which may be consumed in excess), ask your child to drink only water after supper.
■ Avoid serving food and beverages high in caffeine.
■ Talk to your child's doctor about the possibility of constipation or a urinary infection as a contributing factor.
■ Serve low-salt foods in the evening, such as a cookie instead of chips or a rice cake instead of salted popcorn.

HOME COMFORT AND MANAGEMENT TIPS

Stress often accompanies bed wetting, affecting both parents and child. One of the most important tasks in the management of bed wetting is to not add more stress. Make your child more self-reliant and avoid making humiliating remarks or responses to the problem:

- Keep a light on in the bathroom and make sure the hallway is adequately lit.
- Discuss bladder training with the pediatrician. Exercises such as holding urine and stopping the flow once started (as with the Kegel exercises mothers are taught in childbirth preparation classes) may help strengthen control.
- Prepare ahead—cover the mattress with a plastic liner (under bed sheets).
- Leave a change of underwear, clean sheets, or at least a towel so the child can take care of himself when a bedwetting incident occurs.
- Reward dry nights (perhaps with a sticker), but don't punish for the wet nights.
- Reduce stress—avoid scary movies, violent TV shows, very physical exercise, or arguments right before bed.
- Keep your child on a reasonable sleep schedule.
- Do the obvious—make sure your child empties her bladder before bed.
- Reassure your child and the rest of the family that the problem will be outgrown.

RECIPES

HONEY AND 'JAMAS

When I was a little girl, my mother spread leftover scraps of pie-crust dough with honey, folded them into tart shapes, and baked until crispy. When I was baking one evening, my girls asked for the same treat. I told them if they could be in their pajamas by the time the treat came out of the oven, they could have one. They were, and this snack was forever referred to by this silly name.

> *1 prepared pie crust or leftover scraps*
> *Honey*

1. Preheat the oven to 325°F.
2. Cut dough into equal-sized squares at least 3 in. in length and width. Spread one half of each square with honey.
3. Fold each square over into a triangle and pinch the edges to seal the honey in. Prick the top with a fork.
4. Bake for 10 minutes.
5. Eat right away. Don't forget to brush your teeth!

CRISPY OATMEAL COOKIES

YIELD: 2 DOZEN SMALL COOKIES

These are fine cookies to serve after dinner. The inclusion of oatmeal in the recipe appeals to my parental instincts to serve healthy desserts. Unlike many cookie recipes, this one calls for only a little bit of baking soda, and no table salt at all.

> 1 stick (¹/₂ cup) butter
> ¹/₃ cup brown sugar
> ¹/₂ cup granulated sugar
> 1 tsp. vanilla
> 1 large egg
> 1 cup all-purpose flour
> ¹/₂ cup whole-wheat flour
> ¹/₂ tsp. cinnamon
> ¹/₄ tsp. ground nutmeg
> ¹/₄ tsp. baking soda
> 1 cup uncooked oatmeal
> 2 tbsp. milk

1. Preheat the oven to 375°F. In a bowl, beat the butter with the sugar until creamy. Add the vanilla and egg and mix well.
2. In a separate bowl, combine all remaining ingredients, except the milk, and stir. Add the flour mixture and the milk to the sugar mixture; stir it until well mixed. The dough will be crumbly.
3. Drop the dough by spoonfuls onto a lightly greased cookie sheet and bake for 10 minutes until cookies are just golden.

CAVITIES (DENTAL CARIES)

Ninety-five percent of all Americans have cavities, but with good dental care and proper diet, you can at the very least limit the number your child will have. Three conditions are needed to create a cavity: a susceptible tooth, cavity-causing bacteria, and a carbohydrate-containing food, such as a sugar or starch.

Your child's first tooth can appear when she is as young as 4 to 6 months old, and that is when good teeth-cleaning habits should start, too. Cavity-causing bacteria cling to the sticky stuff on teeth that we know as plaque. Proper cleaning and thoughtful food selection can limit the bacteria and their harmful effects. When sugar or starches are eaten, the bacteria in that plaque secrete an acid that dissolves tooth enamel. This acid can be produced for up to 20 minutes even after food is swallowed. Plaque between teeth is thought to produce acid for up to 2 hours after eating. The longer a tooth is in contact with this damaging acid, the more likely a cavity is to form.

Children are at greater risk of developing cavities than adults are because they eat more snacks, increasing the exposure to cavity-causing bacteria. Kids also like candy. In particular, hard candy, which lingers in the mouth, is a food that really promotes cavities. Kids are also the target of most advertising campaigns for sugar-carrying foods: young children see some 30,000 commercials each year, and half of these are for foods and beverages with sugar. Compare that with the fact that most kids don't learn about nutrition until adolescence, and you can see why kids get cavities.

CAVITIES AND THE FOOD CONNECTION

For strong, cavity-resistant teeth, your child needs to eat a balance of protein, vitamins, and minerals, especially calcium and phosphorous. A menu based on the Food Guide

Pyramid (see page 16) will provide this. Children need the right amount of fluoride, too. Fluoride protects against cavities; it is particularly effective in the first 8 years of life, when teeth are developing. If your community's water supply is not fluoridated, a prescription for fluoride based on your child's age and weight must be obtained from the pediatrician. Prescription multivitamins are available with or without fluoride. Fluoride is best absorbed on an empty stomach. However, discourage your child from swallowing fluoride toothpaste: it is possible to get too much of a good thing. Too much fluoride can cause cosmetic discoloration of the teeth.

BABIES AND CAVITIES

Teeth start to grow 6 months after conception, and 32 teeth are actually formed, but not visible, at birth. This makes Mom's diet important—though it is extremely rare to have maternal malnutrition actually effect teeth. The most notorious cause of cavities in infants is prolonged exposure to liquids such as formula or juice. These sweet liquids, when allowed to pool around newly emerging teeth, promote cavity formation. When an infant goes to sleep with a bottle, the problem is even worse: saliva flow slows down during sleep, and saliva is needed to help rinse teeth free of cavity-causing substances. Baby bottle–induced tooth decay can be devastating, even requiring the removal of new teeth. To protect your baby's teeth:

- Give only bottles filled with water before naptime.
- Clean your infant's teeth twice a day with gauze or a damp, clean cloth.

SNACKS AND CAVITIES

Regular brushing is essential to preventing cavities, but careful snack selection and the snack frequency are just as important. For example, after most snacks, bacteria release a cavity-causing acid for up to 20 minutes. A child who eats three cookies all at once will have about 20 minutes of increased acid in his mouth, whereas the child who slowly snacks on her three cookies while playing a game or watching TV can stretch that exposure to 60 or 90 minutes, greatly increasing the chance of cavity formation.

The type of food eaten as a snack matters, too. Though sugar is thought to be the worst culprit, it may be that all starchy foods—even cereals and breads (which also contain carbohydrates)—could be as harmful. On the other hand, foods containing fat and protein may counter the effects of the bacteria in plaque. Fat seems to coat the teeth, decreasing sugar solubility, and it may be toxic to the bacteria that promote tooth decay. Protein increases the buffering ability of saliva, also reducing cavity formation.

Foods high in fiber, such as apples and celery, may be better snack choices because they increase saliva production, which washes away lingering food debris.

To reduce the risk of cavities:

- Limit the number of times your child snacks in a day.
- Ask your child to brush or at least rinse with water after each meal or snack.
- Examine the type of snacks your child eats. Foods containing some fat or protein may be good between-meal snacks at school when brushing is difficult. These include cheese, nuts, or other foods from the meat, poultry, fish, dry bean, eggs, and nuts group. Plain yogurt, milk, and fruit—either fresh or packed in water—are thought to be good snacks, too.
- Foods such as popcorn, soda crackers, hard rolls, pretzels, corn chips, or even pizza are less likely to promote cavities than are cookies, sweet rolls, pies, and cakes.
- Most vegetables, including celery, sliced carrots, pepper rings, or cucumbers, are good between-meal snack choices.

■ Limit liquid snacks, such as juice, soda, or chocolate milk. Liquids can bathe a tooth in sugar, even depositing it between teeth. When trying to reduce cavities, remember that water is the best between-meal beverage.

■ Sticky foods, such as raisins and gummy-type candies, are poor snack choices because of their sugar content and their ability to cling to surfaces.

SUGAR AND CAVITIES

It is impractical to eliminate all forms of sugar. Sugar is found in nutritious foods like bananas, beets, melons, and peaches, not just in sweets. Even such sugars as the lactose in milk or maltose in grains can contribute to tooth decay. Catsup, peanut butter, and salad dressings often contain it even though they don't taste sweet. What does need to be controlled is the amount of time a tooth is exposed to the acid that is formed once the sugar is eaten:

■ After eating sugar or carbohydrate foods, brush teeth.

■ Eat sugar-containing foods with meals instead of as a snack.

■ Read food labels and compare sugar content. Each 4 grams of sugar equals 1 teaspoon.

■ Use the Food Guide Pyramid (see page 16). The concentration of sugar symbols can help guide you to the low-sugar food groups.

HOME MANAGEMENT TIPS

It is usually recommended that your child's first visit to the dentist be around his third birthday. If you are phobic about dental visits, try not to pass your fears to your child. Find a dentist who specializes in kids; ask other moms or your pediatrician. You are likely to find that going to the dentist is a much more pleasant experience for kids today than it was for you. Ask your dentist to teach your child how to brush and floss properly. In most cases, parents have to brush their childrens' teeth until the children are at least 6 years old. Ask your dentist about using colored disclosing tablets. Have the kids brush and then give them one of these colored tablets as directed on the package. The tablets will dramatically color any remaining food and plaque, easily identifying any shortcomings in your child's brushing techniques.

If your child has an alarming number of cavities, start keeping a food diary (see the example on page 24). Keep a diary for 7 days. Look at the quality of her diet: does it approximate the Food Guide Pyramid? (See page 16.) What about snack frequency and type of snacks? Keep track of brushing, too. Use the food diary as a tool to identify the cause of cavities.

Here are more methods for fighting cavities:

■ Encourage your child to brush twice a day for approximately 2 minutes. Try using a kitchen timer or one from a family game to demonstrate how long 2 minutes really is.
■ Set a good example yourself with regular brushing.
■ Get children into the habit of flossing when they're young.
■ Ask your preschool or day-care center to sponsor a dental hygiene education day. Kids really listen to their teachers at these early ages.
■ Ask your child to rinse with water after meals if brushing isn't practical at school.
■ If necessary, offer your kids sugarless gum when they can't brush. Try a gum sweetened with the sugar substitute Xylitol. Xylitol increases saliva flow and helps in the fight against microbes. A 1989 Report by the American Dental Association reported when kids were given xylitol-sweetened gum, they had fewer cavities than kids who chewed other gums. Don't give gum to children under age 4.

RECIPES

FRUIT 'N' NUTS

YIELD: 2 SERVINGS

Foods that are good for kids often aren't kids' favorites. Not so with this great snack combo. There's no *added* sugar in this snack, but brushing or rinsing after eating is still advised.

> *2 tbsp. no-sugar-added peanut butter*
> *1 tbsp. sesame seeds, chopped peanuts, or pecans*
> *1 large ripe pear (or a crisp apple)*

1. Cut the pear in half. Leave the skin on, but carve out the seeds, making a small indentation.
2. Fill each hole with half the peanut butter and sprinkle with the nuts. Serve right away.

RAINBOW SALAD

YIELD: 2 SERVINGS

In today's world fruits and vegetables have to compete with heavily advertised, fancily packaged snacks. Moms and dads can help even out the competition by preparing fruit in a colorful manner as described here. I find that my kids don't ask for fruit often, but when I put a bowl of Rainbow Salad in front of them, it disappears.

> *1/2 cup of any three of the following: seeded watermelon,*
> *cantaloupe, honeydew melon, banana, kiwi, strawberries,*
> *blueberries (cut into 1/2-inch cubes)*
> *1 cup plain or vanilla yogurt*

1. In 2 clear glass bowls or even wine goblets, place a layer of 1 type of fruit, topped by 1/4 cup yogurt, then another layer of fruit, then another 1/4 cup yogurt, and finish with the remaining fruit.
2. Serve right away.

CUCUMBER BOATS

YIELD: 2 BOATS

These snacks are fun to look at and eat. The cottage cheese filling provides a bonus of calcium for building strong teeth.

1 small cucumber, peeled
1 tbsp. onion, finely minced
¹/₄ cup cottage cheese
Paprika or parsley for garnish (optional)

1. Cut the peeled cucumber in half. Using a spoon, scoop out the seeds, making a hole about ¹/₄ in. deep.
2. Mix the onion with the cheese and blend well.
3. Fill each half of the cucumber with the cottage cheese mixture and sprinkle with a bit of the garnish on top for color. Serve right away.

SWISS POTATOES

YIELD: 2 SERVINGS

This is a fine snack to serve your kids on cold, wet days. It is based on a traditional Swiss recipe. Use whatever cheese your child likes. At our house, Sarah loves Swiss, and Emily, sharp cheddar.

> *2 small, round russett or Idaho potatoes, peeled*
> *2 oz. sliced cheese (Swiss, cheddar, Muenster, mozzarella)*

1. Preheat the oven to 325°F. Boil the potatoes—whole—in water for 10 to 15 minutes or until they are soft when pierced with a fork. Don't overcook them or they will fall apart.
2. Remove potatoes from the pot and pat them dry with a paper towel. Cut the potatoes in half and set them on a lightly oiled baking sheet, with the flat, cut side facing up. Place ¹/₂ ounce of cheese on each potato. Cut or tear the pieces of cheese so that they fit on the top and don't hang over.
3. Bake potatoes in the oven until the cheese melts but does not burn—about 5 minutes. Serve right away.

✎ CHICKENPOX (VARICELLA)

There are over 3 million cases of chickenpox each year in the United States, 90 percent of which occur in children under 15 years old. The good news about chickenpox is that the first infection will almost always provide your child with a lifelong immunity.

Chickenpox usually shows up as bumps on the face and trunk 10 to 20 days after exposure to the virus. In some cases, a fever, usually within the first 3 days, or respiratory symptoms can proceed an outbreak. The telltale lesions can occur all over the body, even in the scalp, nose, mouth, and intestine, where fortunately, they are asymptomatic. New chickenpox lesions stop erupting after 5 to 7 days.

In most cases, your pediatrician is likely to prescribe only comfort measures. Use acetaminophen for pain relief, cool soaks for itching, and plenty of rest. Benadryl may be recommended to help with symptoms and promote sleep. Do not use aspirin because it increases the risk of Reye syndrome.

Keep the lesions clean and try to keep your child from scratching. Serious complications from chickenpox are rare in children unless there is a secondary infection, such as if one of the sores gets irritated and infected. Help prevent this by keeping fingernails short and hands clean. In some cases, the medication acyclovir (Zovirax) is prescribed for kids with a weakened immune system, but in general, prescription drugs are usually not required. Although complications in children are rare, hospitalization is sometimes required and kids with serious illness, such as cancer or human immunodeficiency virus (HIV) can become dangerously ill when infected with chickenpox. Also, chickenpox becomes a significant source of lost wages in families in which both parents work away from home. For these reasons, a vaccine has been developed; in the near future, it is likely to become a part of routine medical care.

CHICKENPOX AND THE FOOD CONNECTION

In the overwhelming majority of cases, chickenpox is self-limiting, clearing up on its own within days or a week of the first symptoms. If your child has a fever, his need for fluids will increase and so will his need for calories. Don't be surprised if the pain and discomfort caused by the itchy lesions temporarily rob your child of his appetite. To meet energy needs, your child will pull from her own nutrition stores. If the lesions are in her throat or mouth, it will become important to serve bland, soft, cool foods. Spicy, highly flavored foods can be irritating. While your child has chickenpox, food becomes a source of comfort, so offer a regular supply of fluids but, feel free to indulge her desire for even unusual foods:

■ Allow your child to eat the foods that satisfy his appetite.
■ Instead of sticking to a regular meal schedule, offer a steady supply of small snacks.
■ Offer a tasty supply of fluids. Juices like cranberry or apple are good choices. Do not give your child citrus fruits or juices if she has lesions in the mouth.
■ Offer soda if the carbonation does not irritate your child's mouth. Serve regular soda, not diet; chances are he will need the calories real soda carries.
■ Soft foods may be very appealing. Read about soft, bland foods on page 229 in Chapter 4. In addition to the recipes that follow Home Comfort and Management Tips, try the Macaroni and Cheese recipe on page 238, the Chunky Applesauce recipe on page 250, and the recipes for milk and yogurt shakes on pages 132 and 245.
■ Custard and milk-based puddings are a great source of calories and protein. They are also bland and easy to swallow. If your child is not eating regular meals serve the custard or puddings in Chapter 4 (see pages 247–49) as temporary meal replacements.

HOME COMFORT AND MANAGEMENT TIPS

Ask your doctor about the proper medications for treating symptoms. Most pediatricians suggest the use of Aveena Oatmeal Baths, which provide temporary relief of itching. Be careful when getting your child out of the tub, as the oatmeal makes it very slippery. Topical hydrocortisone cream is not recommended for itching. Ask the doctor about the use of calamine lotion, or try an ice pack on really itchy spots. Other tips:

- Trim your child's fingernails and tell her not to scratch.
- Keep your child out of the sun. Sunburned lesions may lead to scarring.
- Dress your child in loose clothing.
- Notify your doctor if lesions appear to be infected or symptoms such as fever or vomiting persist.

RECIPES

EGGS IN A HOLE

YIELD: 1 PORTION

This recipe is traditionally prepared by dads on camping trips. When my Sarah came down with chickenpox and had very little appetite, David made this for her. The egg-and-toast combination is appropriately bland and the right serving size when appetites are not robust.

> *1 slice of bread, white or whole wheat*
> *1 egg*
> *1 tbsp. grated mild (American or Muenster) cheese (optional)*

1. Cut a 2-in. circle in the bread. If your child does not like crust, trim it off.
2. Place the bread in a lightly buttered frying pan on medium heat. Break the egg into the hole and cook for about 1½ minutes, then turn it with a spatula and cook it on the other side.
3. Sprinkle the cheese on the egg before serving. Serve warm.

FISH IN A BLANKET

YIELD: 1 SERVING

Looking for something appealing to serve in bed or on the couch that won't be messy? Try this fun variation on a tuna sandwich.

> *¹/₂ cup prepared tuna*
> *2 slices fine-grain bread (white bread usually works best)*

1. Trim the crusts from the bread.
2. Using a rolling pin, roll each bread slice, so that it is very thin.
3. Spread an equal amount of tuna on each slice. The tuna must be as smooth as possible.
4. Then roll up each slice to create a miniature sandwich roll. Serve right away or make ahead and keep refrigerated until ready to serve.

FISHERMAN'S PIE

YIELD: 4 GOOD-SIZED SERVINGS

You will be quite taken with the ease it takes to put this dish together. Its creamy, slightly bland flavor and appearance are pluses when only soft foods will do. The whole family will enjoy it, which means Mom won't have to make separate meals for anyone.

> *1 lb. haddock, sole, or halibut fillet, cut into cubes*
> *2 lb. potatoes, peeled and cubed*
> *2¹/₂ cups milk*
> *6 tbsp. butter*
> *¹/₂ cup grated cheddar cheese*
> *6 tbsp. all-purpose flour*

1. Preheat oven to 350°F. Arrange the prepared fish in the bottom of a 2-quart casserole dish that has been buttered.
2. Boil the potatoes in lightly salted water until they are tender.
3. While the potatoes boil, melt 4 tbsp. of the butter in a saucepan, stir in the flour, and cook mixture for 2 minutes. Slowly stir in 2 cups of the milk and cook on medium heat until the sauce thickens. This will take about 7 minutes. Remove from heat and set aside.
4. Drain water from the potatoes and mash them with ¹/₂ cup of the milk, 2 tbsp. butter, and the cheese and set aside.
5. To assemble the pie, pour the sauce over the fish, then top with the prepared potatoes so that all the fish is covered and the potatoes make a crust on top. Cover the pie with aluminum foil and bake for 30 minutes.

VERY BERRY PUDDING

YIELD: 2 CUPS

Puddings are a traditional sick-day food because they are easy to swallow and have a soothing texture. Try this cool, fruit-packed alternative when your child gets tired of custard or even ice cream.

> **2 cups blueberries or strawberries, rinsed and trimmed**
> **2–3 tbsp. sugar**
> **1 cup cold water**
> **2 tbsp. cornstarch**
> **¼ cup whipped cream (optional)**

1. Combine the fruit and 2 tbsp. sugar with 1 cup cold water in a saucepan. Bring to a boil, reduce heat to low, and simmer for 5 minutes.
2. Mash the fruit with a fork or a potato masher until the fruit is in small chunks but not puréed. Taste for sweetness; add the remaining sugar if a sweeter taste is desired.
3. In a small bowl, mix ¼ cup of the cooked fruit with the cornstarch and mix until well combined. Return the cornstarch mix to the remaining fruit.
4. Bring mixture to a boil, reduce heat, and simmer on low for 5 minutes more. Stir frequently to prevent burning.
5. Pour pudding into individual serving dishes or a 2-cup bowl and refrigerate for 60 minutes before serving. It will thicken as it cools. Top with a spoon of whipped cream before serving, if desired.

⤐ CHOLESTEROL

More than 6 million American men and women have symptoms of heart disease. There is evidence that heart disease can begin early in childhood. Cholesterol can accumulate in the arteries, causing atherosclerosis or heart disease, which, after many years, can lead to a heart attack. A diet that contains lots of cholesterol and saturated fats is believed to increase the risk of heart disease.

Cholesterol is not all bad. It is used to make hormones and is needed for proper brain, nerve, and muscle development. Your child needs fat and cholesterol for proper growth, but like most adults, children get 38 to 41 percent of their calories from fat. A level closer to 30 percent is believed to be healthier.

Most children do not need to have their blood cholesterol levels tested, but the pediatrician may recommend a cholesterol test if a parent or grandparent had a heart attack at an early age. Parents with blood cholesterol levels above 240 milligrams per deciliter may want to discuss high cholesterol levels with the pediatrician because the condition can run in families. If the doctor does suspect your child is at risk, she will probably ask him to have a fasting blood test. She will measure not only total cholesterol but also other fats in the blood known as high-density lipid (HDL) cholesterol, low-density lipid (LDL) cholesterol, and triglycerides. This is called a lipid profile and gives more accurate results than testing blood cholesterol alone. A cholesterol reading in children that exceeds 200 milligrams per deciliter is considered high, and 170 to 199 milligrams per deciliter is borderline. If the test results are high, it is not uncommon to repeat the test for accuracy. If the results remain high or even borderline, the pediatrician is likely to start you on a step-one diet. This regimen is very similar to the prudent diet described below under Cholesterol and the Food Connection. It is best to plan this with the help of a registered dietitian. A diet lower in fat called the step-two diet will be implemented after 6 months if cholesterol levels stay above the acceptable levels.

Diet is only one factor in heart disease. Overall health, obesity, genetics, smoking, and exercise are other factors that can effect the risk.

CHOLESTEROL AND THE FOOD CONNECTION

Do not start infants or very young children on low-cholesterol diets. Very young children need a lot of calories to grow properly, and fat is the densest form of calories. Its elimination can stunt growth. Skim or partly skimmed milk is not recommended in the first 2 years of life, specifically because it contains too much protein and sodium to be easily digested and it is too low in calories for proper growth. Wait until your child's second birthday to start giving low-fat dairy products.

The National Cholesterol Education Program recommends a diet with the following characteristics for all kids after age 2: a wide variety of foods, adequate calories for growth and for meeting and maintaining a healthy body weight, saturated fat that amounts to less than 10 percent of the diet, total fat that does not exceed 30 percent of calories; and total cholesterol that does not exceed 300 milligrams. This means that a child requiring 2,000 calories can eat approximately 65 grams of fat and 20 grams of saturated fat per day.

Most of the calories in the diet—55 to 60 percent—should come from carbohydrate foods, and protein should make up 10 to 15 percent of calories. To meet these guidelines, read labels, use the Food Guide Pyramid (see page 16), and follow these simple meal-planning tips:

■ Use lean cuts of meat and poultry.
■ Remove skin from poultry before serving.
■ Bake or broil fish instead of frying.

- After your child reaches age 2, start the whole family on skim or 1 percent milk.
- Use vegetable oils and olive oil for cooking instead of butter or lard.
- Do not automatically add butter or margarine to vegetables, potatoes, or pancakes. Try to help your child develop a taste for these foods without high-fat flavorings.
- Limit egg yolks to two or three per week.
- Do not restrict your child's diet. Serve lots of whole-grain bread and cereals along with plenty of fruits and vegetables.
- Encourage your child to develop a taste for fish. Research suggests fish may contain beneficial oils that help prevent heart disease.
- Limit processed foods, soft drinks, desserts, and candy to prevent obesity.
- Compare labels on snack foods. Each 5 grams of fat in a portion is equivalent to eating 1 teaspoon of butter.
- Keep a food diary (see sample on page 24). Record what your child eats over several days. Compare it to the food group servings suggested in Chapter 1. The food groups on the bottom of the Food Guide Pyramid (see page 16) are lower in fat. Fat content progresses as you reach the top of the Food Guide Pyramid.
- Pay attention to your child's weight. Excessive weight gain indicates your child is eating more calories (probably from fat) and is not getting enough exercise. Do not start your child on restrictive weight-loss diets. Read about children and weight control on pages 259–60 in Chapter 5.

HOME MANAGEMENT TIPS

A prudent diet is only one part of a healthy life style for your child. Regular exercise, avoidance of smoking, and regular medical checkups are important, too. Some other good practices include:

- Keep TV viewing to a minimum. In a 1992 University of California study, excessive TV watching was the greatest predictor for a child with a high cholesterol above 200 milligrams per deciliter. It was found that kids who watch a lot of TV have dietary and physical activity habits that lend themselves to higher cholesterol levels. Children are averaging 3 hours of TV watching per day, an amount that exceeds all other activities in which they participate.
- Teach your kids how to read a label. Use food labels to become familiar with the fat and saturated fat content of food.
- Become familiar with the snacks and lunch served at school.
- Set a good exercise example. Find an activity to do with your kids.

RECIPES

FRIENDLY FRIES

YIELD: 2 GOOD-SIZED SERVINGS

Kids love French fries! Deep frying destroys most of the vitamin C they contain and adds lots of fat that few kids need. In our house, we love these low-fat French fries that are baked, not fried. I usually leave the skins on for extra fiber.

> *4 Idaho or russet potatoes, peeled or unpeeled and cut into*
> *¹/₄-in.-thick French fries*
> *1 tbsp. canola oil*
> *salt to taste*

1. Preheat oven to 400°F. Place the prepared potatoes in a glass bowl and pour the oil over them. With a wooden spoon, gently toss the potatoes several times so that each piece is coated with oil.
2. Spread the potatoes on a baking sheet. Bake them for 10 minutes in the preheated oven. With a spatula, turn the potatoes so that all sides brown, then continue cooking for 10 minutes more. The potatoes should be golden brown.

FRUIT IN A CLOUD

YIELD: 4 SERVINGS

Meringue baskets do look like soft, puffy clouds. They are a dessert that parents can feel good about because they contain only a tiny amount of fat—and in this version, a good helping of fresh fruit. This tastes particularly yummy with strawberries or fresh peaches. I have also made it with cut-up kiwi, banana, and pineapple. If the fruit is very tart, you will need to sweeten it with a bit of sugar.

> *2 cups fresh fruit, peeled, seeded, and cut into bite-sized pieces*
>   *(sprinkled with 1 tbsp. sugar if desired)*
> *2 egg whites*
> *Pinch of salt*
> *5 tbsp. sugar*
> *Waxed paper to line the baking sheet*

1. Preheat the oven to 225°F. Beat the egg whites until they start to foam, add the salt, and then beat in the sugar. Continue beating until the egg whites form very stiff peaks.
2. Place a sheet of waxed paper on a baking sheet. Drop a quarter of the egg-white mixture onto the wax paper. Using a spoon, shape the egg whites so that they have an indentation in the center to hold the fruit—like a small bird's nest.
3. Bake baskets for 2 hours until the meringue is firm and dry. Remove the clouds and let them cool before filling them with the prepared fruit.

BUTTERMILK BANANA BREAD

YIELD: 2 LOAVES

This makes a great snack and breakfast treat. Freeze one loaf for the next time your child wants something delicious and healthy to snack on, and eat the other right away!

3 egg whites
1 egg
^{1}/$_2$ cup mashed banana
1 ^{1}/$_2$ cups brown sugar
3 cups sifted all-purpose flour
^{1}/$_2$ cup oatmeal
2 tsp. baking soda
^{1}/$_4$ teaspoon salt
2 cups buttermilk

1. Preheat the oven to 350°F. Lightly oil two 4″ × 8″ loaf pans.
2. Beat the egg whites, egg, and banana together. Add the sugar and mix until well blended.
3. Combine all the dry ingredients and add to the banana mixture, alternating with the buttermilk until all the ingredients are well combined. Do not overmix.
4. Pour the batter into the prepared pans and bake the bread for 1 hour. It is done when a knife inserted in the center comes out clean.

☙ COLDS (UPPER RESPIRATORY INFECTIONS)

As a parent, you can expect your young child to get three to eight colds each year, tapering off to two or four a year as he gets older. Colds start to become common at 3 to 4 months of age. Because a cold causes a stuffed-up nose, difficulty feeding is often the first sign in infants; older children often have less desire for food or fluids. A cough and fever can sometimes accompany a cold, but not always. Sleepiness, vomiting, and even conjunctivitis can all be companion symptoms, too.

The average uncomplicated cold is supposed to disappear in 3 to 5 days, but a recurrent runny nose is not uncommon, either. If your child is in overall good health, a runny nose without any of the other symptoms listed above is likely to be annoying but not harmful. Kids are more likely to get colds because they do not yet have the antibodies to fight off all cold viruses. Day care and cold weather increase the risk of catching colds because more kids carrying the cold virus come into contact with one another. The best way to prevent colds in infants is to keep them away from people who have the virus. A dry house, dust, smoke, and allergies are all factors that can make cold symptoms worse.

There is no cure for the common cold, so prophylactic antibiotics are never needed. Your pediatrician may recommend acetaminophen for pain relief. Prolonged use of vasoconstrictor nasal drops—for more than 7 days—can cause a rebound effect, oral decongestants can cause jitters in children, and antihistamines can make children drowsy. These are some of the reasons most pediatricians will not advise the use of cold or cough medicines for children under age 3.

If your infant is under 6 months old, you should carefully observe your baby's cold symptoms because infants can get into respiratory trouble faster than older kids. The pediatrician can advise you on what symptoms require medical treatment. Call the doctor if your older child has difficulty breathing, complains of ear pain, or has a temperature of 102°F or over. The prognosis for a cold is usually excellent, but colds lower resistance in the nose and throat, allowing secondary infections of the sinus or eye. A cold can even progress to pneumonia. If a cold lasts more than 2 weeks, especially if it is accompanied by a cough, call your doctor. If your child is excessively sleepy or cranky, call the doctor then, too.

COLDS AND THE FOOD CONNECTION

There is no way to prevent a cold, but diet can reduce the number of colds your child might have in a year and a diet rich in vitamin C may limit the duration of symptoms. When a cold does take hold, a menu that includes plenty of fluids can give relief.

NUTRITION AND COLD RESISTANCE

Since an ounce of prevention is worth a pound of cure, try keeping your child's body well nourished. Of course, all nutrients are essential, but the nutrients that fortify the immune system include protein, vitamins C and A, and iron. It is also critical that your child eat enough food—that is, enough calories to meet the demands for growth and fighting illness. If your child is a very picky eater, consider a children's multivitamin mineral supplement.

VITAMIN C AND THE COLD

In 1994, the Center for Science in the Public Interest, a consumer health advocacy group, looked at the efficacy of vitamin C in preventing colds. A review of 12 carefully designed studies showed that vitamin C, even when given in doses that exceed the U.S. RDA, did not prevent colds. A few studies, however, did show that vitamin C was capable of reducing the severity and duration of symptoms. A 1981 study conducted on identical twins in Australia found that 1,000 milligrams of vitamin C given daily reduced the duration of cold symptoms from 6½ days to just over 5 days. In these cases, the vitamin C was taken before symptoms appeared. Dosages of 1,000 milligrams per day for children are not recommended because the long-term effects have not been studied. In some cases, large doses of vitamin C have caused kidney stones. The best way for your child to get the appropriate amount of vitamin C is from the food you give her.

Vitamin C cannot be stored, so the body saturates tissues with as much vitamin C as it can keep and then excretes the excess. The body pulls from these stores to fight infection and is dependent on a new supply every day for replenishment. To get the beneficial effects of vitamin C, give your child a superb vitamin C source twice a day during cold season. All fruits and vegetables contain some vitamin C, but the ones listed here are particularly rich in this nutrient:

▪ Fruit: cantaloupe, grapefruit or grapefruit juice, kiwi, orange or orange juice, papaya, strawberries, tomatoes or tomato juice
▪ Vegetables: broccoli, green leafy vegetables, green peppers

PLENTY OF FLUIDS

More than half of your child's weight is made up of water. His natural thirst mechanism is usually adequate to meet his need for fluids, but it is not perfect, and during illness, he may have less interest in eating or drinking. When he has a cold, offer plenty of fluids, but don't force them, either. Just make sure they are available and in a form that is likely to be consumed. Try the following suggestions:

▪ Serve a glass of water or fruit juice with each meal or snack.
▪ Warm soup is a great fluid source and it also soothes a dry throat. The steam really can clear nasal passages, too.
▪ Many people do not serve milk or milk-based soup or beverages for fear they will increase mucus production. Results of recent scientific studies do not bear this out. Since milk shakes or even cream soup can be very comforting for sick little ones, do not automatically avoid these foods.
▪ Fresh fruit, such as juicy watermelon or grapefruit sections, are a good source of fluid.
▪ Serve fruit-flavored gelatin; 1 cup provides the body with as much liquid as 1 cup of water.

HOME COMFORT AND MANAGEMENT TIPS

Here are more tips for fighting colds and making your child comfortable:

▪ Use a cold-mist humidifier in your child's room to ease breathing.
▪ Put a pan of water on the radiator or wood stove.
▪ Have your child take a warm shower to loosen nasal secretions and aid breathing—try this before naps or bedtime.
▪ To loosen nasal secretions in infants, give them a warm bath before using a suction bulb. Infants have a very tough time feeding with a stuffed-up nose, so try a bath before feedings, too.
▪ Put ChapStick or petroleum jelly around nostrils to prevent or soothe skin made sore from blowing.

■ Practice teaching young children how to blow their nose before they get a cold. Put a tissue or feather on your hand and ask them to blow it off with their mouth closed. Another effective technique is to press one nostril closed with a finger and blow out the other.

■ Keep toothbrushes separate when a cold is lingering in the house—get a new toothbrush every few months anyway.

RECIPES

GRANDMA'S CITRUS TEA

YIELD: 2 QUARTS

This is the perfect beverage for summer colds, but it can be pressed into use in the winter, too. This makes a large batch, but I promise the whole family will make it disappear. Just make sure the child with the cold gets some, too!

> *3 tea bags (orange pekoe works well)*
> *6 cups cold water*
> *1 6-oz. can frozen orange juice*
> *1 6-oz. can lemonade*
> *1 medium orange, sliced*
> *1 lemon, sliced*

1. In a clear plastic or glass pitcher, steep the tea bags in 6 cups of cold water. Leave it sitting in the sun until it is the color of cream soda. This will take about 60 minutes.
2. Stir in the frozen juice concentrates and the fruit slices. Place it in the refrigerator for 20 or 30 minutes. Serve over ice.

FLORIDA EGGNOG

YIELD: 1 SERVING

Here two nourishing ingredients are combined to make a drink that kids enjoy and moms can serve as a good meal replacement. Egg substitute is used instead of raw egg to eliminate the risk of food poisoning, but it is still a good protein provider.

1 cup orange juice
1 tbsp. sugar
1/4 cup egg substitute
Crushed ice
Orange slice for garnish

1. Combine all ingredients in a blender. Purée until smooth.
2. Garnish with an orange ring (or maybe even a cherry!). Serve right away.

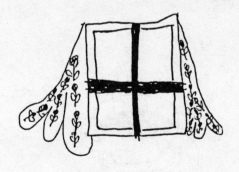

SWEET GARLIC SOUP

YIELD: 6 CUPS

Soup and garlic both fight colds. When garlic is cooked, it is not strong-flavored, but sweet and soothing.

> *10 large garlic cloves, peeled and sliced thin (about ¹/₂ cup)*
> *1 small onion, peeled and sliced into thin rings*
> *2 tbsp. butter*
> *6 cups chicken broth*
> *1 tbsp. fresh lemon juice*
> *¹/₂ cup croutons for garnish (optional)*

1. In a heavy soup pot, sauté the garlic and onions for 2 minutes until they are soft, but do not let them brown.
2. Add the chicken broth and simmer on low heat for 30 minutes.
3. Purée mixture in a food processor, then return it to heat.
4. Stir in the lemon juice, cover, and simmer the soup for another 60 minutes. Serve soup warm, with a few croutons floating on top.

⤚ COLD SORES (ORAL HERPES)

These small, painful blisters appear on the edge of the lip at unpredictable times. They are caused by herpes virus type 1, which is similar to, but not the same as, herpes simplex virus type 2, which causes genital herpes. Children get the virus by direct contact with the sore or through saliva. An outbreak usually lasts about 7 to 10 days, then the blister dries, scabs, and heals over. The virus remains dormant until it resurfaces. Herpes simplex type 1 is very common. By age 15, eight out of 10 people carry the virus, though fewer than half actually develop the blisters. In young children, an outbreak will usually appear by age 4 if the child carries the virus.

Fever, poor health, and stress are all thought to act as outbreak triggers. There is no cure for the condition; the blisters will heal by themselves without complications as long as children don't pick at the scabs. Your pediatrician may recommend an ointment such as camphorated phenol for comfort.

COLD SORES AND THE FOOD CONNECTION

If fever accompanies a herpes outbreak—and sometimes it can—a child may be more irritable and less interested in eating. Some parents believe they can identify trigger foods that bring on an outbreak. This is highly individualized. Here are some tips about food and cold sores:

▪ If the sores inhibit eating and drinking, try serving cold liquid meals, such as fruit or ice cream shakes.
▪ Have your child use a straw to avoid irritating sore spots.
▪ Avoid acid foods, such as tomato products or citrus fruits and juices.
▪ Try offering slightly bland, creamy foods, such as soup or casseroles.

LYSINE AND COLD SORES

Lysine, an amino acid found in protein-containing foods, has long been touted as a herpes inhibitor. Research in the early 1980s suggested that large concentrations of lysine inhibit the herpes virus, particularly when intake of another amino acid, arginine, is kept low. But a review of the research in a 1984 issue of Nutrition and the M.D. found that in a double-blind placebo-controlled study using 1,000 mg of lysine per day, the amino acid had no effect on the prevention or healing of herpes sores. Even if lysine had been found to be effective, lysine supplements should not be given to children. A single dose of one amino acid, such as lysine, may block the absorption of other essential amino acids, creating a nutritional imbalance. Though lysine has not been shown to be effective in the treatment of herpes, eating foods rich in lysine and low in arginine is not hard to do. Such foods include cheddar cheese (lysine, 2,072 milligrams per 3.5 ounces; arginine, 941 milligrams per 3.5 ounces), Atlantic cod (lysine, 1,390 milligrams per 3 ounces; arginine, 906 milligrams per 3 ounces), milk (lysine, 650 milligrams per cup; arginine, 290 milligrams per cup), and poultry (lysine, 2,200 milligrams per 3 ounces; arginine, 1,560 milligrams per 3 ounces). A diet based on the Food Guide Pyramid (see page 16) could easily supply 1,000 milligrams of lysine per day.

HOME COMFORT AND MANAGEMENT TIPS

Cold sores are painful, unattractive, and contagious. Your child may feel self-conscious when a blister appears. It will help if you explain its cause and instruct your child to keep it clean and dry. Remind him that it will soon disappear. Comfort measures include the following:

■ Try a cool compress on the lip, or a wet, cool tea bag.
■ Put sunscreen on your child to prevent sunburns, which are thought to trigger the virus.
■ Try lubricants such as petroleum jelly for comfort.

RECIPES

FOG SOUP

MAKES 6 SERVINGS

The potato is my idea of a good sick-day food. A child will find potatoes pleasingly bland, subtle, and easy to swallow when they're cooked in a soup.

> *1 small leek, very well scrubbed and minced*
> *1 small yellow onion, minced*
> *2 tbsp. butter*
> *3 medium-sized potatoes, peeled and diced*
> *3 cups chicken broth*
> *1 13-oz. can whole evaporated milk*

1. In a heavy soup pot, sauté the leek and onion in the butter until they are tender but not brown. Add the potatoes and the chicken broth and cook the mixture on medium heat for 20 minutes. Do not let it boil.
2. In a food processor, purée the entire mixture and return to the pot. Stir in the canned milk. Reheat on low heat for 5 minutes. Serve warm.

CHICKEN WITH A HAT

YIELD: 4 SERVINGS

In this recipe, the "hat" is a biscuit crust. It covers the whole top, sealing in flavor and keeping the chicken very moist and tender. This dish is creamy, warm, and mildly flavored. It is a very soothing recipe.

1 cup diced, cooked chicken
3 tbsp. butter
3 tbsp. all-purpose flour
1 1/2 cups milk, warm
3 oz. grated cheddar cheese
1/2 cup cooked carrot coins
Biscuit topping (directions below)
2 cups all-purpose flour
3 tsp. baking powder
1/2 teaspoon salt
4 tbsp. soft butter
1 cup cold milk

1. In a medium saucepan, melt the butter, stir in the flour, then cook the mixture for 2 minutes.
2. Stir in the milk and cook on medium heat until it starts to thicken (about 5 minutes).
3. Add the cheese, then stir in the chicken and the carrots. Pour the mixture into a lightly buttered soufflé or casserole dish.
4. Preheat the oven to 375°F.
5. Make the biscuit topping: combine the dry ingredients. With clean fingers, mix in the butter until it is well distributed and the flour has taken on a grainy quality. Pour in the milk and blend with a spoon.
6. Drop spoonfuls of the dough on top of the chicken pie so that the entire top is covered. Bake in the preheated oven for 25 minutes. Serve warm.

VERY VANILLA

MAKES 1 SERVING

Gourmet coffeehouses have sprung up across the country like dandelions on a spring day. These stores carry flavored syrups intended for coffee but superb for children's beverages. Add them to milk or ice cream or use them to make frozen drinks. The vanilla syrup in this drink gives it a truly intense flavor.

> ½ cup *French vanilla ice cream*
> 1 cup *milk*
> 1 tbsp. *vanilla syrup*

1. Blend all ingredients in the blender until smooth. Serve right away. Garnish with grated chocolate if desired.

⌇ COLIC

Don't be too surprised if, in the third week of her life, your sleepy little infant begins a pattern of unexplainable crying. Up to 30 percent of newborns do. If your infant is under 3 months old and cries 3 hours per day, 3 days per week, then she meets the definition of infantile colic. This upsetting behavior usually manifests itself in the early evening: a calm, placid infant can suddenly start crying for no obvious reason, her face becoming red and knees drawn up to her abdomen as if in pain. These episodes can last from 10 minutes to 2 hours and are a great source of stress to Mom and Dad, but they are largely unexplained by the medical profession. Fortunately, by the time babies are 3 months old, the problem usually stops.

Most pediatricians explain colic as the result of a newly functioning digestive tract. It may be that an intestinal spasm is the cause or that food intolerance is a factor. Crying itself may fill the stomach and intestine with air, causing crampy pains that lead to even more crying. If the infant burps, passes gas, or has a bowel movement, the crying may stop—for the moment. There is also an emotional component to colic: it is most likely to occur in first-born infants, suggesting that experience in parenting somehow eliminates the colic.

Lots of research has been done to find a cure for colic. So far, the passage of time is the only true treatment for the condition. An infant who cries for long periods of time should always be checked by a physician, but once it is ascertained that there is no medical cause for your baby's misery, your pediatrician is likely to offer only reassurance that the condition will pass. On some occasions, sedatives or antispasmodic medications may be prescribed by the pediatrician before feedings. The use of beer, wine, or alcohol has no place as a relaxant for infants.

COLIC AND THE FOOD CONNECTION

Cow's milk, formula, and even mother's milk have been identified as factors in colic symptoms. If there is a history of cow's milk allergy in your family, then your infant may have the allergy, too, and a formula made from cow's milk might cause a reaction that shows up as colic. Other signs of food sensitivity, such as skin rashes and sniffles, usually accompany true cow's milk allergy. Breast-feeding mothers may have colicky infants because they themselves eat and drink dairy products. It is the protein and the naturally occurring antibodies carried in milk and related foods that could pass from the mother's food to her breast milk and to the infant, where it is the cause of colic. Both breast-fed and formula-fed infants experience colic. Even infants on soy-milk formula instead of cow's milk formula can have colic. Switching formula types can alleviate symptoms temporarily, but if the colic is not due to true allergy, symptoms will recur. For this reason, changing formulas frequently to treat colic is not routinely advised.

Stopping breast-feeding is never a recommended treatment for colic. Breast-feeding mothers do not need to switch to a bland, boring diet, either. Studies suggest that mothers who eat a varied and well-seasoned menu actually have infants who like to nurse more. Excessive intake of some foods, such as garlic and onions, might be problematic for some infants, but this is highly individualized. Even chocolate and coffee in reasonable amounts have not been found to cause colic.

What can help both infant and parents is a regular feeding schedule. Though feeding infants on demand is recommended over a rigid feeding schedule, a flexible but established schedule can prevent a chaotic feeding routine that might intensify colic symptoms. If your baby is colicky, take the following steps:

- If you suspect cow's milk formula as a factor in your infant's symptoms, discuss it with the doctor. Soy-milk formula is as nutritious as cow's milk formula and is effective in some cases.
- If you are breast-feeding and consuming a lot of dairy products, a temporary reduction in the amount of milk, yogurt, or cheese you eat might yield positive results. Be sure to eat nondairy calcium sources (see chart on page 186).
- Breast-feeding mothers may find limiting caffeine beverages to two per day (this includes coffee and cola drinks) may be beneficial.
- Keep a diary of your infant's feeding schedule. This will help you begin and maintain a routine and prevent over- or underfeeding. It will also give you reassurance that your infant isn't starving.
- Ask your pediatrician or nurse about the type of bottle nipple and the size of the hole best for your baby's age. Sucking on an air-filled bottle or a bottle that flows slowly might cause more air to be swallowed and cause coliclike symptoms.
- Burp your baby after every feeding.
- OTC colic remedies such as Mylicon drops are available at all pharmacies. Ask your doctor if these preparations are appropriate for your baby.

HOME COMFORT AND MANAGEMENT TIPS

There is no one treatment for colic, and some methods work only on occasion, but experiment with them all and take comfort in knowing your baby will outgrow the problem. Though crying is extremely stressful to parents, it is one of the things babies do with great regularity. Measures to try include the following:

- Call your doctor or nurse. Studies show that reassurance from the baby's health-care providers is the best coping tool for parents.

- If you are in a crisis, call your local hospital's maternity ward and speak to a nurse.
- Mothers need some rest. Find a way to get help in the evenings when crying is most likely to occur.
- Carry your little one in the football hold: allow your forearm to support the body, stomach side down, head in your hand, and legs dangling.
- Burp your baby.
- Try a pacifier.
- Sit in a rocker with your infant; try wearing earphones connected to the TV or radio or stereo to keep you relaxed.
- Take a walk with the baby in the stroller.
- Take a car ride with the baby in the infant car seat.
- Turn on gentle music or use a vacuum or radio to provide white noise.
- Do not overstimulate with lots of toys, colors, sounds, or people.

✎ COUGH

Though annoying and sometimes alarming, a cough is actually useful and offers protection against more serious respiratory infections. A cough is a reflex action intended to clear the airway of irritating secretions or even objects and material. Sinusitis and postnasal drip are common causes of a cough. Second-hand smoke and allergies can cause coughing as well.

Any persistent cough warrants a call to the pediatrician. A cough that goes away with sleep may have a psychological basis. Medication may be recommended in some cases: if a cough interferes with sleep, a cough suppressant may help; coughs due to allergies can be helped with antihistamines; and a night cough due to asthma may be helped by bronchodilators. Discuss the use of medications with your health-care provider.

Croup is characterized by a deep, barking cough. It is caused by a virus and usually but not always effects children under age 3. Mild croup can be managed at home, but discuss treatment with the pediatrician, particularly if breathing is difficult.

COUGH AND THE FOOD CONNECTION

Coughs will self-extinguish once the underlying cold or allergy symptoms resolve. In the meantime, increased fluid intake can help in several ways: (1) fluids can help loosen phlegm, making it easier for the cough to clear the airway; (2) fluids can also keep the mouth and throat well lubricated, giving these irritated areas a bit of comfort and relief; (3) and warm fluids also can calm irritations. In our house, alternating with warm and cold liquids has been helpful in treating a persistent cough.

Some good cough remedies include the following:

▪ At each meal and snack, offer your child a glass of water or juice.
▪ Serve special drinks, such as the fruit shakes in Chapter 4 (see pages 245). Kids will often drink more of a "special" beverage.
▪ In an attempt to break a daytime coughing jag, try alternating a warm liquid—such as those suggested under Warm Liquids on page 243 or even warm tap water—with a cold drink such as a milk shake or even a dish of ice cream or sherbet.
▪ For kids over 1 year of age, try a teaspoon of honey to coat the throat.

HOME COMFORT AND MANAGEMENT TIPS

Adding humidity to your house is often a useful recommendation. A dry house adds to the coughing problem. Measures for making your child more comfortable include the following:

- Use a cool-mist humidifier daily. Clean the humidifier each night to destroy harmful bacteria or fungi.
- Lower your home's temperature.
- In New England, cold, fresh air is considered a traditional antidote to illness. Though the science is not well explained, leaving a window cracked allows cool, moist air in, which many find helpful in reducing the cough reflex.
- Try elevating the head of your child's bed at night. This may help reduce postnasal drip and the nighttime cough associated with it.

RECIPES

HAWAIIAN SLUSH

YIELD: 3 CUPS

This recipe is a favorite in our house when a cough lingers on and on. The cold, refreshing fruit and fizzy bubbles offer a bit of relief, or at the least, a little distraction.

> *2 cups canned, unsweetened pineapple chunks; reserve the juice*
> *1 cup ice cubes*
> *Seltzer water*
> *1 cherry or an orange slice for garnish*

1. Drain the fruit and reserve 1 cup of the juice.
2. In a blender, purée the fruit with the juice.
3. Fill a tall glass with ice. Pour half of the fruit purée on top of the ice. Stir and fill with enough seltzer water to fill to the top of the glass.
4. Refrigerate the remaining purée for use in a drink later.

BLUE BUBBLE SALAD

YIELD: 2 CUPS

Gelatin salads are a dish I remember fondly from my childhood in the 1950s. Today, they don't seem so popular with adults, but kids still love them. The blueberries float like giant bubbles in the ginger ale gelatin. This is a delicious way to push fluids.

> *1 tbsp. unflavored gelatin*
> *2 cups ginger ale*
> *1/2 cup frozen whole blueberries*
> *Whipped cream for topping (optional)*

1. Sprinkle the gelatin over 1/4 cup of the cold ginger ale. Don't stir, but let it soak in for 3 minutes.
2. In a saucepan, bring 1/2 cup of the ginger ale to a boil.
3. Remove the pan from heat and stir the gelatin into the hot ginger ale until it is dissolved. Stir in the remaining ginger ale and the blueberries.
4. Pour the mixture into a glass bowl and chill, until firm, for 2 to 3 hours. Top with a bit of whipped cream before serving.

⟫⟩⟩ CONSTIPATION

Chronic constipation accounts for 3 to 5 percent of pediatric office visits. It is common in the first year of life and particularly between the ages of 2 and 4. It is slightly more common in girls, and there may be a genetic component, meaning it affects entire families. Some babies, even in the first weeks of life, pass harder, firmer stools than other babies. Because diet is not yet a factor at this early age, it may be that these kids are just prone to constipation.

Constipation is usually defined as hard, painful stools, not just infrequent bowel movements. The frequency of bowel movements in infants and children can vary tremendously. Some healthy breast-fed infants might have a bowel movement only once a week, while other children have them three times in a day. If your child is having a bowel movement less often than you think he should, this does not necessarily mean he has true constipation. Discuss the problem with your pediatrician.

In some cases, a child can develop a crack in the skin of the anus, called an anal fissure. Because the fissure can bleed and be painful after a bowel movement, it is not unusual for a child to try to withstand the natural urge to defecate. The result can be constipation. It is also possible that a serious underlying condition, such as an intestinal abnormality, is the cause, but in the majority of cases, the common causes of constipation are dietary. If your child has constipation, discuss it with the doctor to rule out any medical problems; a program of increased fiber, fluids, and exercise is likely to be the prescription. In children under age 2, a suppository or a lubricated rectal thermometer may be used to stimulate a bowel movement; and in older kids, mineral oil—even manual disimpaction by the pediatrician—may be needed. Stool softeners may also be prescribed.

Encopresis, a condition in which stools are passed involuntarily, can result from constipation. One percent of 5-year-olds have this problem, which may be related to toilet training. Though encopresis was once thought to be caused by psychological factors, results of new studies show that psychological reasons are not the primary cause. A careful program that includes laxatives, lubricants, and a high-fiber diet is usually required for treatment.

CONSTIPATION AND THE FOOD CONNECTION

The dietary factors that cause constipation in kids include dehydration, lack of fiber, and too much cow's milk. Fruits and vegetables are superb fiber and fluid sources, but 75 percent of American kids eat less than the recommended amounts they need for good health. Cow's milk is a great protein and calcium source, but it contains virtually no fiber. Because it is dense in protein and calories, it can replace the desire for high-fiber foods.

CONSTIPATION AND FIBER

The AAP suggests a fiber intake of 0.5 grams of dietary fiber per kilogram of your child's body weight, up to a maximum intake of 20 to 35 grams a day. Christin Williams, M.D., director of the child health center in Valhalla, New York, recommends the "age + 5" rule for determining fiber: After age 2, increase fiber to an amount equal to or greater than their age plus 5 grams per day. Eight grams of dietary fiber would be appropriate for a 3-year-old, 25 grams for a 20-year-old. If your child is constipated, she will need to reach that upper 20- to 35-gram limit but don't exceed that amount. Proceed with caution: too much fiber too fast can cause gas and bloating.

Children who were constipated as infants should eat natural fiber sources once they start on solid foods. Start serving fresh or cooked fruit once your child is 6 months old. In the beginning, peel and seed fruits, because these are

FIBER CONTENT OF FOODS (IN GRAMS)

Cereals:

40% Bran Flakes, 1/2 cup	3.7
Kellogg's Raisin Bran, 1/2 cup	2.6
All-Bran, 1/3 cup	8.8
Bran Buds, 1/3 cup	7.8
Puffed rice, 1 1/2 cup	0.3
Shredded wheat, small biscuits, 1/2 cup	2.5
Cheerios, 3/4 cup	1.2
Kellogg's Corn Flakes, 3/4 cup	0.3
Kix, 3/4 cup	0.6
Wheaties, 3/4 cup	1.8
Cooked oats, 1/2 cup	1.9
Spaghetti, 1/2 cup	0.9
White rice, 1/3 cup	0.5
Brown rice, 1/3 cup	1.6
Wheat Germ, 3 tbsp.	4.1

Beans:

Kidney beans, 1/3 cup	3.8
Lentils, 1/3 cup	2.6
Baked beans, 1/4 cup	2.9

Vegetables:

Frozen corn, 1/2 cup	3.4
Peas, 1/2 cup	4.1
Potato, 3 oz.	2.5
Acorn squash, 3/4 cup	5.3
Snap beans, 1/2 cup	2.0
Broccoli, 1/2 cup	2.5
Raw carrots, 1 cup	3.6
Cauliflower, 1/2 cup	2.0
Mushrooms, 1/2 cup	3.1
Pea pods, 1/2 cup	2.7
Raw tomatoes, 1 cup	1.4

Bread:

Whole wheat, 1 slice	1.5
White, 1 slice	0.5
Pumpernickel, 1 slice	3.8
Wheat tortilla, 1–6 in. in diameter	0.8
Corn tortilla, 1–6 in. in diameter	2.7

Fruit:

Apple, 1	2.1
Banana, 8 in.	2.2
Raw cherries, 12	1.4
Grapes, 15	0.7
Orange, 1 small	2.0
Canned pears, ½ cup	2.8
Dried figs, 1½	4.0
Raisins, 2 tbsp.	1.2

hard to swallow, but by the time your baby is 8 months old, she can eat soft, ripe fruits with skins. Also offer at least one small serving of cooked vegetables each day, but hold off on the corn until your baby is 8 or 9 months old, because some kids have trouble digesting it. Though white-rice infant cereal is most common, brown-rice infant cereal tastes just as good and carries a bit more fiber. When you start offering crackers and bread, try giving your baby whole-wheat bread, oatmeal bagels, or bran muffins. Don't use All-Bran or fiber supplements as a means to increase the fiber in your baby's diet. Always give your infant something to drink along with meals.

To add more fiber to your child's diet:

- Serve whole-grain breads, such as rye, pumpernickel, whole wheat, oatmeal, and bran. Serve whole-grain muffins, rolls, and crackers.
- Work in extra fiber with breakfast cereals. Wheaties, Nabisco Shredded Wheat, Cheerios, and oatmeal-based cereals are all good choices.
- After your child is 1 year old, serve at least two whole fruits and two to three vegetables every day. See Chapter 1 (page 7) for recommended serving sizes to match your child's age. When possible, leave the skins on. Canned fruits packed in natural juices are a convenient alternative to fresh fruit.
- Serve beans frequently. Just ½ cup of baked beans carries 7 grams of fiber. Children often enjoy beans in soup or chili or mixed with pasta. Mexican bean dip served as a snack or as a bean burrito is a great fiber source.
- For snacks, try nuts or popcorn (not for infants or very young children).
- Sprinkle 1 teaspoon of wheat bran or wheat germ over cereal, yogurt, or ice cream. Because wheat bran is a concentrated fiber source (12 grams per ounce), do not give

your child large amounts of it. Too much bran can cause digestive disturbances.

▪ Try serving your child Dr. Boodish's No-Fail Constipation Cure on page 113. The combination of dried fruit makes it very rich in fiber.

▪ Ask your pediatrician about using one of the fiber supplements available at the supermarket and drugstore. They include Hydrocil, Metamucil, Naturacil, Fiberall Wafers, and Fibermed Snacks. Follow the package instructions carefully.

▪ When adding fiber to your child's menu, be sure to encourage him to drink plenty of fluids, too. Encourage him to drink water or juice at each meal and with between-meal snacks, too.

NATURAL FOOD LAXATIVES

You should *never* give your child laxatives—and you never really need to, because there are a few foods that could be called Mother Nature's laxatives. These include prunes, Karo syrup, mineral oil, dried fruit, and unprocessed bran:

▪ *Prune juice* is a time-honored laxative. Prunes carry two chemicals, isatin and phonophthalein, which are thought to act as natural stimulants to the intestine. Try serving your child prunes or prune juice. If she does not like these, try fresh plums or Plum and Yogurt Parfait (see recipe on page 131).

▪ *Karo syrup* is an intensely sweet carbohydrate that may help relieve constipation by increasing the speed food exits from the stomach. Pediatricians often recommend adding a teaspoon of Karo syrup to an 8-ounce bottle to help loosen stools.

▪ *Mineral oil* is a widely recommended lubricant. The findings of a 1939 study suggested that mineral oil could negatively effect vitamin absorption, but findings of more recent studies do not support this. Use it based on your doctor's recommendation.

■ *Tomatoes and tomato juice* are recommended as a natural lubricant.
■ *Unprocessed bran* combats constipation by absorbing water and forming bulkier, larger stools.

HOME COMFORT AND MANAGEMENT TIPS

Constipation can be common in the toilet-training years. Kids may withhold a bowel movement because they do not want to soil their garments or they are just too busy to take the time to go to the bathroom. If the urge to defecate is ignored, it will go away, and constipation can result. Four-year-olds are not likely to use the toilet unless reminded. Set a schedule, particularly before leaving the house, and ask your child to at least sit on the toilet. If he goes, fine; if he doesn't, hope for the best. Do not get into a struggle over toilet training—it will eventually be accomplished! To encourage regularity:

■ Establish a bathroom pattern. You cannot make your child have a bowel movement, but you can help her by setting aside time to use the toilet.
■ Try a sitz bath if your child has an anal fissure.
■ Encourage some regular activity. Most little ones don't need much encouragement on this score, but lack of exercise can be a factor in regularity, particularly in older kids.

RECIPES

DREAM BEAN DIP

YIELD: 1½ CUPS

This is a delicious way to add fiber to your child's diet. Use it as a dip as suggested here or roll it in a warm, soft tortilla, add some grated cheese, and you have a great burrito.

> *1 medium onion, finely chopped*
> *1 clove garlic, finely chopped*
> *1 tbsp. butter*
> *1 16 oz. can kidney beans, rinsed and drained*
> *1 tbsp. chili powder (optional)*
> *¼ cup grated cheddar or Muenster cheese*

1. In a frying pan, melt the butter and sauté the onion and garlic until soft and translucent (about 2 to 3 minutes).
2. Add the beans. With a wooden spoon, mash all the beans into the onion mixture until somewhat smooth. Add the chili powder if you wish.
3. Stir in 1 tbsp. water. Continue cooking the mixture for another 5 minutes to allow time for flavors to blend.
4. Sprinkle with cheese and serve as a dip with tortillas.

CHA-CHA CHILI

YIELD: 4–5 CUPS

The goodness of this dish relies on simmering, to blend flavors. Bulgur gives it a meaty texture and replaces some of the meat traditionally used when making chili. Bulgur is an inexpensive source of fiber and minerals.

1 medium onion, chopped
2 cups water
2 cloves garlic
1 tbsp. canola oil
¹/₂ lb. ground beef or ground turkey
2 16-oz. cans kidney beans, drained and rinsed
¹/₂ cup bulgur (available in most markets or health-food stores)
1 28-oz. can crushed tomatoes
1 medium carrot, scrubbed
3 tbsp. chili powder

1. In a large soup pot, sauté the garlic and onion in the oil for 3 minutes.
2. Add the ground meat and cook another 3 minutes. Drain fat.
3. Stir in the kidney beans, bulgur, tomatoes, carrot, chili powder, and 2 cups of water. Cover and cook for 20 minutes. Test to see if the bulgur and carrots are cooked. Cook another 10 minutes if necessary. Serve warm.

BLACK-MAGIC BROWNIES

YIELD: 1 DOZEN BROWNIES

The first time I made these brownies, I conducted the ultimate test: I served them to my girls and to our young neighbor, Kiele Raymond. They loved them and asked for more. From this successful taste test, I knew that the unusual addition of black beans did not interfere with the traditional brownie flavor.

1 16-oz. can of black beans, rinsed and drained
2 oz. unsweetened chocolate
4 tbsp. butter
3 large eggs
$^1/_2$ cup brown sugar
$^1/_2$ cup granulated sugar
$^1/_4$ cup all-purpose flour
$^1/_2$ tsp. baking powder
2 tbsp. corn syrup
1 tsp. vanilla extract
$^1/_2$ cup chopped nuts (optional)

1. Preheat the oven to 350°F. In a food processor fitted with a steel blade, purée the beans until they're smooth. In a small saucepan, melt the butter and chocolate, then add this to the bean mixture. Purée for 30 seconds.
2. Add all remaining ingredients, except for the nuts, to the bean mixture. Turn on the food processor and blend for 1 or 2 minutes. The mixture should be smooth and all ingredients well combined. The batter will be thin. Blend in the nuts with a spoon.
3. Pour the batter into a lightly oiled 8" × 11" brownie pan and cook for 20 minutes. For a thicker brownie, use a 9" × 9" cake pan and cook for 25 minutes. To test for doneness, insert a knife into the center of the brownies. When the knife comes out clean, they are ready.

ALPHABET STICKS

YIELD: 10 STICKS

Whole-wheat bread is not always a favorite with kids because it is coarser and heavier than white bread. To get your kids to eat more whole grains, try this recipe. These bread sticks can be shaped into your child's own initials, and he can easily help you with making the letters.

> 2 cups whole-wheat flour
> 1 tbsp. brown sugar
> 3¹/₂ tsp. baking powder
> 1 cup milk
> ¹/₃ cup melted butter

1. Preheat the oven to 350°F.
2. In a large bowl, mix the whole-wheat flour with the sugar and baking powder. Stir in the milk and blend until all ingredients are combined.
3. Gather the dough into a ball and gently knead it on a floured board for 2 minutes.
4. Roll the dough on a floured board into an 8″ × 12″ rectangle. With a sharp knife, make 10 strips 8 in. long.
5. Dip the strips into the melted butter, then shape them into the desired letters and place them on a baking sheet.
6. Cook in a preheated oven for 18 minutes or until lightly browned. Serve right away—plain or with jam or honey.

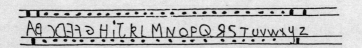

DR. BOODISH'S NO-FAIL CONSTIPATION CURE

YIELD: 4 CUPS

When constipation is a problem, turn to this good-tasting natural laxative. The combination of prunes and figs make this an intensely fiber-rich food. Serve it as a topping on cereal, as a dessert with a little whipped cream, or on toast as a jam.

> *1 cup pitted prunes, chopped*
> *1 cup figs, chopped*
> *1 cup raisins*
> *1 cup water*
> *2 tbsp. chopped apricots (for tartness)*

1. Combine all the above ingredients with ⅓ cup of boiling water.
2. Stew for an hour, adding more water if it gets too thick. It should have the consistency of preserves.
3. Cool and refrigerate.

DARK, SWEET BRAN MUFFINS

YIELD: 12 MUFFINS

Bran flakes and dried fruit make this a good fiber source; molasses and brown sugar make it flavorful. Serve these muffins for breakfast as a tasty way and nutritious way to start your child's day.

¹/₂ cup whole-wheat flour
1 cup white flour
¹/₂ tsp. salt
1¹/₂ tsp. baking soda
2¹/₂ cups unprocessed bran
¹/₂ cup finely chopped prunes or raisins
2 large eggs
¹/₂ cup brown sugar, packed
¹/₄ cup molasses
1¹/₂ cup sour milk (to make sour milk, add 1 tbsp. white vinegar to each cup of milk and allow to sit for 10 minutes before using)
2¹/₂ tbsp. melted butter

1. Preheat the oven to 400°F. Sift together the flour, salt, and baking soda. Add the bran and dried fruit to the flour mixture.
2. Mix together the eggs, sugar, molasses, milk, and butter. Pour into the flour mixture. Stir with a wooden spoon until all ingredients are combined, but do not overmix.
3. Pour the mixture into lightly greased muffin pans. Bake 20 minutes. Remove from the tins and serve warm or cold.

DIARRHEA

Diarrhea is the body's way of ridding itself of an irritating or harmful toxin. There can be many causes of diarrhea, including viruses, bacteria, parasites, and infections of the ear or urinary tract. Diarrhea may be caused by allergies, but the connection is not well established. It might even be a case of overeating or ingesting too much of one type of food, such as fruit juice.

Diarrhea presents a significant risk for dehydration for children under 6 months old. Your pediatrician should be consulted if your infant has diarrhea or if there is blood or mucus in her stool. Though diarrhea is annoying and alarming, parents should not automatically try to suppress it with medications. Diarrhea is usually self-correcting.

A common side effect of antibiotics can be diarrhea. When given for months, antibiotics might harm friendly intestinal bacteria, with diarrhea being a side effect. Alert your pediatrician if your child suffers this side effect, as a change in medication may eliminate the problem.

An increasingly frequent but unexplained phenomenon in American children is known as chronic nonspecific diarrhea, or sloppy stool syndrome. The typical patient is young—6 to 20 months old, and has three to six mucousy stools during the day. The diarrhea is not associated with any other symptoms and these children appear healthy and happy and grow normally. The condition may be caused by abnormal bile acid absorption (bile acid is a substance that works on dietary fat) or incomplete carbohydrate absorption. Spontaneously, usually at age 3½, the problem resolves. Fifty percent of children with nonspecific diarrhea have a similarly effected sibling. The pediatrician investigates to rule out underlying and potentially serious problems, such as malabsorption, but this investigation usually comes up empty. A varied diet that does not include excessive clear liquids can help improve symptoms, but by age 4 complete recovery is expected.

Traveler's diarrhea can be a concern to parents whether traveling out of the country or across state lines. Anytime you travel to new regions, a change in eating routine and water source increases the risk of diarrhea. It may be caused by unfamiliar bacteria or a virus. In most cases it is merely annoying, not life threatening. If traveling out of the country with a child to a place where the risk of diarrhea might be greater, ask your pediatrician about antidiarrheal medicines. A pediatrician may not recommend bismuth subsalicylate (Pepto Bismol) because it is similar to aspirin and, like aspirin, might be linked with Reye syndrome. In some cases where it is not easy to get medications or the risk of bacterial infection is considered great, it may be wise to request, before your departure, a supply of antibiotics for use in an emergency. Discuss your plans for travel with your pediatrician and get specific advice regarding which OTC and prescription medicines to carry.

DIARRHEA AND THE FOOD CONNECTION

The treatment for diarrhea has traditionally been a menu of diluted formulas, clear fluids, and bland foods, such as rice and bananas. Evidence from several new studies suggests that a mixed diet of varied foods is just as successful in treating diarrhea as is a restrictive menu. Fluids are always needed.

DIARRHEA AND FLUIDS

A general guideline for fluid needs during a bout of diarrhea is 2 ounces of fluid every hour for infants and 4 ounces every hour for older children. If your pediatrician recommends a clear-fluid diet, offer the drinks listed below. Do not use a clear-liquid diet for more than 24 hours without discussing it with your pediatrician—it is not adequate in calories or nutrients. Do not overdo fluids, either. Inappropriate continuation of clear liquids might even promote loose stools. Water given to infants instead of formula for extended periods can lead to water intoxication. In some cases, the pediatrician may recommend oral rehydration therapy, a fancy name for liquids that contain salt and minerals. Products like Pedialyte might be suggested; follow the doctor's recommendations regarding their use.

Some forms liquids can take include the following:

▪ Clear fluids include clear broth; bouillon; cranberry juice; apple juice; grape juice; gelatin (not diet); ice water; Popsicles; clear, weak tea; defizzed clear, carbonated soda, such as ginger ale (defizz soda by leaving its container open or shake the bottle before pouring and let it sit a minute or two before drinking).
▪ Ice pops or crushed ice topped with fruit juice can be a nice way to serve fluids, particularly if your child has a fever and his appetite is poor.
▪ Weak, warm tea sweetened with honey (for children over age 1) and a pinch of salt may be a pleasant fluid for some kids. (Honey shouldn't be given to babies because it could contain a bacteria that can cause infant botulism.)

FRUIT JUICE AND DIARRHEA

Fruit juices, particularly apple and pear juice, have been known to cause diarrhea when consumed in excess. Results of a recent study suggest that some kids absorb white grape juice better than apple juice. If your child has unexplained diarrhea, try restricting fruit juice and fruit drinks for 2 or 3 days. Serve only one 4-ounce glass of vitamin C–containing fruit juice each day, but let your child drink as much water as she wants and the recommended amount of milk for her age. Continue to serve fruit—up to two or three servings—just hold back on the juice. If the diarrhea stops, excessive juice consumption was probably the cause. Try giving white grape juice, too. Most kids like it, but excessive amounts could cause diarrhea.

MILK AND DIARRHEA

Diarrhea can cause a temporary intolerance to the milk sugar lactose. The intestinal villi, fingerlike projections that help in the digestion of lactose, can be damaged during bouts of diarrhea, causing a temporary inability to digest milk. If the diarrhea is prolonged, secondary intolerance to sucrose (white sugar) can develop, too. If you suspect temporary milk intolerance:

- Try a temporary lactose-free diet (see page 183).
- Yogurt with "live cultures" may be beneficial. The fermenting process predigests some of the lactose, making it more digestible even when lactose intolerance is a problem. Plus, the natural bacteria may help re-establish a balance in the intestine that can help correct diarrhea.

THE BRAT DIET

The scientific rationale behind the BRAT diet, a time-honored remedy of bananas, rice, applesauce, and toast, may not be very well documented, but this combination of foods is thought to have binding effects. These foods are also generally well tolerated, making them good sick-day or transitional foods when going back from liquids to solids.

BRAT

My children were very young—about 12 months old—when their pediatrician first recommended the BRAT (bananas, rice, applesauce and toast) diet to treat diarrhea. To take some of the boredom out of the limited menu, I came up with several combinations my kids liked—yours might, too:

- Mash cooked rice with very ripe bananas.
- Serve puffed rice cereal with apple juice instead of milk.
- Cook white rice in apple juice instead of water.
- Spread toast with mashed bananas.
- Make an applesauce sandwich. Remove crusts from white bread and spread it with applesauce. Cut it into strips.

NONSPECIFIC CHRONIC DIARRHEA

Parents may try to treat nonspecific chronic diarrhea problem with a lot of different dietary changes and manipulations. One pediatric medical manual states that a low-fiber, low-fat, high-sugar diet may make the condition worse. If you suspect your child has this problem:

- Observe your child's meal and snack schedule. If she is not on a three-meal, two-snack schedule, try starting her on this schedule and see if it has any effect on her bowel movements. Select snacks that come from one of the main food groups—not from the fats, oils, and sweets group.
- Limit fruit juices for a trial period.
- Do not add high-fat foods to your child's diet, but do let him eat foods that contain a natural source of fat, such as lean meat, poultry, fish, cheese, and other dairy products.

- Foods rich in water-soluble fibers, such as oatmeal, barley, pears, and apples, may help slow food transit time through the intestine and help ease the diarrhea symptoms.
- Avoid snacks with a high sugar content. Read the product label: if the words *sugar, sucrose,* or *high-fructose corn syrup* occur as one of the first five ingredients, the product is likely to contain too much sugar.
- Frequent between-meal snacks and chilled fruits may escalate the problem.
- Read about milk and diarrhea, above. Avoid milk only if it makes problems worse.
- Monitor your child's weight. If weight loss occurs, discuss it with your pediatrician and ask for a referral to a registered dietitian for nutritional counseling.

DIARRHEA AND TRAVEL

If you are traveling to an area where the risk of diarrhea is high, practice the following safe eating techniques:

- Drink only bottled or canned drinks, including water.
- Do not use tap or well water for washing food, brushing teeth, or drinking.
- Do not use ice.
- Take along water-purifying tablets or boil water.
- Don't eat raw fruits or vegetables.
- Eat only well-cooked food.

HOME COMFORT AND MANAGEMENT TIPS

Good hygiene is essential to preventing diarrhea. Make your child wash her hands after using the toilet—at home and at school. Handle diarrhea as follows:

- Persistent diarrhea can cause sore bottoms. Warm, frequent baths can give relief.

- When traveling, carry towelettes for hand washing and a supply of clean drinking cups.
- Before traveling out of the country, contact your state health department and inquire about the need for shots and preventive treatment for the country you are visiting.
- Uncontrolled diarrhea can be scary for children. If your child has had diarrhea, keep him home until it is resolved.

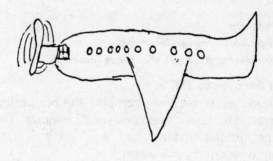

RECIPES

RICE-SO-NICE

YIELD: 4 SERVINGS

This dish can be assembled with ease and baked while you tend to your sick child. It will be ready when you need it and tastes good when reheated, too.

> *1 cup white rice*
> *2¹/₂ cups prepared chicken broth, hot*
> *1 carrot, peeled and cut into thin slivers (optional)*

1. Preheat the oven to 350°F.
2. In a 1-quart casserole dish, combine the hot broth, rice, and carrots. Stir, cover, and cook for 35 minutes. The rice should be soft and tender.
3. Fluff with a fork and serve warm.

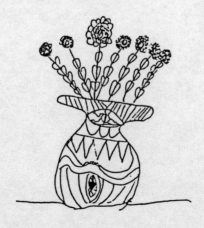

BARLEY SOUP

YIELD: ABOUT 4 CUPS

Barley has very high protein value. I find my kids love these little round grains. This is exactly the soup you will want to serve when little else is tolerated or appealing.

> **3 cups prepared chicken broth**
> **^{1}/$_2$ cup diced carrots**
> **^{1}/$_2$ cup pearl barley**
> **^{1}/$_2$ cup cooked, shredded chicken (optional)**

1. In a saucepan, bring the broth to a simmer.
2. Add the carrots and the barley. Cook for 25 minutes. Taste for doneness. The barley should be very soft and tender.
3. Stir in the chicken if you are using it, and allow the soup to heat through for 3 or 4 minutes before serving. Serve warm.

APPLE PUDDING

YIELD: 2 SMALL SERVINGS

This pudding is easy. It is another simple way to serve apples when your child is sick, and tired of applesauce.

> **1 cup peeled, seeded, cubed apple**
> **^{1}/$_2$ cup apple juice**
> **1 tsp. cornstarch or quick cooking tapioca**

1. Combine all the ingredients in a small microwave-safe bowl. Cook, covered, on high heat for 3 minutes.
2. Stir and let rest covered for another 3 minutes before serving.

BAKED APPLES

YIELD: 1 APPLE

Baked apples should always have a sprinkle of cinnamon and a teaspoon of brown sugar on them. With the help of a microwave oven, this apple dish can be ready to eat in 6 minutes.

> *1 tart apple (Cortland or Macintosh are popular at our house), cored*
> *1 tsp. brown sugar*
> *Dash of cinnamon*
> *1 tbsp. water or apple juice*

1. Put the cinnamon and sugar inside the apple where the core once was.
2. Place the apple in a small microwave-safe dish. Pour the water or juice over the apple. Cover and cook the apple on high for 3 minutes.
3. Let it rest with the cover on for 3 minutes before serving. Serve warm.

BANANA-FANA-FO-FANA

YIELD: 1 SERVING

Bananas are sweet and soft, making them a good sick-day food. They can certainly be served fresh, but when baked, their flavor becomes even sweeter.

1 medium banana with the skin on

1. With a fork, prick a few holes in the banana's skin. Bake the banana in a preheated oven at 325°F for 10 to 15 minutes or in the microwave on high for 3 minutes. The skin will turn brown.
2. Remove the banana from the oven. With a spoon, scrape the banana from the peel.
3. Serve right away in a small dish or combine with hot cereal as a very soothing sweetener.

OATMEAL WITH FRUIT SAUCE

YIELD: 3 CUPS

This is an old-fashioned sick-day remedy. Perhaps it is the soluble fibers contained in the oatmeal and fruit that give comfort to the digestive tract.

3 cups water
2 tbsp. brown sugar
1½ cups rolled oats
2 apples or 2 pears, peeled, cored, and chopped

1. Bring the water to a boil. Add 1 tbsp. of the brown sugar, then stir in the oats. Reduce the heat to low and cook the oatmeal for 10 minutes.
2. In a microwave-safe dish, combine the fruit, remaining brown sugar, and 1 tbsp. water. Cover and cook in the microwave for 3 minutes. Mash the fruit into a purée.
3. Serve the oatmeal warm and topped with a generous spoonful of fruit.

✼ EAR INFECTION (OTITIS MEDIA)

By age 3, two thirds of American children will have had at least one ear infection—some, three or more. It is the most common diagnosis among children under 15, and it is on the rise. Doctor's office visits for ear infections were up 150 percent between 1975 and 1990, particularly in kids under age 2. Infants who get an ear infection in the first 2 to 3 months of life are more likely to have recurrent bouts later on, and this starts a distressing, seemingly endless cycle of antibiotic therapy.

Children get ear infections because the eustachian tube that drains fluid from the ear to the back of the throat is short and horizontal. (In adults, the tube is longer and tilts downward to the throat.) Fluid gets trapped in the tube, and if germs multiply in this sticky fluid, infection or inflammation can result.

There is no clear explanation for the rise in ear infections. Some experts believe that physicians diagnose it more quickly because of improved equipment; others suggest that in the absence of life-threatening ailments like polio and measles, doctors now have more time to identify and see patients with ear infections.

Otitis media (inflammation of the ear) is the collective name for ear infection and fluid in the middle ear. The condition can be acute, chronic, and with or without symptoms. Acute ear infection is accompanied by pain and often fever, and the child is likely to be agitated. In otitis media with effusion, which means there is fluid in the ear but not infection, there are often no symptoms at all.

Not only do ear infections often hurt, they can also cause hearing loss, which, in young children, can delay speech and language development as well as effect performance in school. Otitis media is not contagious. It can be caused by both bacteria and viruses, though bacteria is the most common cause.

In an acute ear infection, a 7- to 10-day course of antibiotic therapy is usually effective. Side effects linked with antibiotics include allergic reaction, stomachache, diarrhea, and skin rashes. Some of these side effects can be prevented by carefully following the label instructions regarding food or liquids. However, fears of drug-resistant antibiotic bacteria are real and are causing doctors to rethink aggressive use of antibiotics whenever possible. Traditionally, when fluid had built up in the ear, antibiotics were prescribed in hopes of preventing an infection. New guidelines put out by the U.S. Department of Health and Human Services and the Agency for Health Care Policy and Research suggest doctors consider a "wait and see" approach when treating asymptomatic fluid in the ear. It is reported that 60 percent of these cases will resolve within 3 months without treatment, and 85 percent within 6 months. If your pediatrician follows the new guidelines, it may mean that when your child has fluid in the ear but no sign of infection, no treatment will be prescribed. Instead, the ear will be re-examined in 3 months. If the fluid is still there and there has been no hearing loss, the doctor may again wait and see. If there is a hearing loss or signs of infection, antibiotics are likely to be prescribed.

EAR INFECTIONS AND THE FOOD CONNECTION

When ear infections repeatedly effect a child, parents naturally want to find a way to stop the cycle. Diet and nutrition can be a factor, but not a cure or treatment.

How you feed your newborn can effect her chances of developing ear infections. Mothers who breast-feed their babies for at least 4 months give their babies more protection against ear infections. Bottle-feeding increases the risk of ear infection two to three times.

The relationship between allergy and ear infection is unclear. Allergy can cause increased mucus production from the nose and clog the eustachian tube, preventing drainage and increasing the risk of infection. If you suspect a food allergy, try to identify it. A short-term elimination of a food could help to rule out or confirm it as a factor. Do not eliminate whole food groups or your child may become undernourished. To help reduce the risk of ear infections:

- Breast-feed your infant for at least 4 months, preferably longer.
- If bottle-feeding your infant, do not prop the bottle upright. Such a position may cause a reflux of fluid into the eustachian tube, and this has been a suspected factor in ear infections among bottle-fed babies.
- Follow the recommended feeding schedule for introducing foods to infants (see page 6). This will assure adequate nutrition and reduce the risk of allergy.
- If your child likes yogurt, encourage its consumption. Select a yogurt with "live cultures," which may help resist infections. Try offering a yogurt shake instead of a full meal (see recipe on page 132).

HOME COMFORT AND MANAGEMENT TIPS

In the beginning phase of an ear infection, children may need more rest and pain management:

- Give acetaminophen as recommended by your pediatrician.
- Try a warm compress on the affected ear.
- If possible, keep your infant out of group day care. Children cared for in their own home have fewer ear infections because they have less contact with germs that can cause illness.
- Do not expose your child to second hand smoke. Contact with smoke increases the risk of ear infections and delays their resolution. Results of a 1994 study concluded at the Rochester School of Medicine and Dentistry, showed that kids with frequent ear infections and children who

are exposed to smoke are at a greater risk of repeating kindergarten or first grade.

▪ Give your child all of the prescribed dose of antibiotics. This can help reduce the risk of antibiotic-resistant bacteria.

▪ Keep your child's doctor informed of alternative medical treatments used to treat ear infections. Chiropractic, holistic, naturopathic, and homeopathic methods have been used by parents in the fight against repeat ear infections. The panel that wrote the 1994 Clinical Practice Guidelines for the treatment of otitis media with effusion recognized that parents turn to alternative treatments. In an attempt to evaluate these programs, literature searches were made and schools of education in the relevant fields were contacted, but results of controlled studies were not adequate to make a recommendation on their use. The panel did find that some of these therapies are without much risk and are inexpensive.

RECIPES

PLUM AND YOGURT PARFAIT

YIELD: 1 SERVING

Here is a dessert Mom and Dad can feel good about because it combines two nutritious foods—fruit and yogurt. Toddlers and older children alike will enjoy it.

> **2 plums, about 2 in. in diameter, any color or variety**
> **¹/₂ tsp. corn syrup (optional)**
> **¹/₂ cup plain or vanilla yogurt**

1. Wash plums and place in a microwave-safe dish. Prick skins and cook on full power for 3 minutes.
2. Let plums cool before handling, then remove peel and pits. Purée or mash the fruit with a fork. Add the corn syrup if the fruit tastes sour.
3. In a pretty serving dish, pour the plum sauce over the yogurt and serve.

FRUIT YOGURT SHAKE

YIELD: 1 SERVING

Yogurt provides a pleasantly flavored alternative to milk-based drinks. In some cases, yogurt may be better tolerated than milk.

> *1 cup plain vanilla yogurt*
> *1 cup fruit juice—orange, raspberry, or cranberry*

1. Purée ingredients in a blender.
2. Serve shake over ice.

⤜ FEVER

Fever is your child's ally when she is ill. It is believed that fever fights infection by stimulating white blood cell production and speeding up the defense mechanisms that promote healing. Acute viral infections are the most likely causes of fever, but others include bacteria, poison, and even drugs. Though any fever can be alarming, the height of the fever is not an indicator of the severity of the underlying cause.

Fever is defined as 1°F above what is considered normal body temperature. Most of us think of normal as 98.6°F, but normal can actually range between 97°F and 100.5°F. New parents are often surprised to learn that a temperature of even 101°F is not much cause for alarm. To most physicians, temperatures above 103°F become cause for concern. However, in children under 3 months of age, a temperature above 100.4°F rectally warrants a call to the doctor.

Your child's body temperature will be lowest between 3 and 6 A.M., and highest between 5 and 7 P.M. Body temperature increases slightly after nursing, eating, or physical activity. None of these factors cause fever, but their ability to raise temperature temporarily can prevent getting an accurate temperature reading.

Most children handle fevers fine; parents are generally advised to let the condition run its course with no treatment. Providing comfort, in the form of rest and tepid baths, is the usual recommendation. Acetaminophen may be advised for pain relief. Children's liquid ibuprofen has recently been approved for use in the treatment of fever, but it remains a secondary choice to acetaminophen.

If your child has a history of fever accompanied by seizures or convulsions, you will need to have specific treatment guidelines developed by the pediatrician. Do not give food or drink during a convulsion. Because infants are at increased risk of dehydration and their bodies don't localize an infection well, the physician should be notified if your infant has a fever and is under 3 months of age. Signs of dehydration in infants include pale skin, dry tongue, thirst, listlessness, rapid pulse, sunken eyes, and a sunken soft spot (fontanel).

FEVER AND THE FOOD CONNECTION

Adequate intake of fluids and calories and comfort are the feeding goals when fever is present. Your child's need for fluid will increase to replace fluid lost through skin, lungs, and body heat. If diarrhea or vomiting are present, fluid losses will be even greater. Fever increases a child's metabolic rate and often robs him of his appetite, making weight loss a likely side effect. For your infant, ask the pediatrician about your baby's need for additional water. For your older child, try to offer enough fluids—about 2 to 4 ounces of fluid per hour—so the urine runs clear. Fluids can take the form of gelatin, ice chips, or liquids. Diet tips for the feverish child include the following:

- Offer cool drinks, not hot; these are better tolerated.
- If your child will tolerate them, supply calorie-containing clear juices or defizzed soda (defizz soda by leaving off the top of its container).
- Freeze soda or juice to make flavored ice chips.
- Serve liquid meals like fruit shakes or yogurt shakes if your child will tolerate them.
- Offer solid, bland foods (see pages 229–30)—they may be better tolerated.

HOME COMFORT AND MANAGEMENT TIPS

Try to make your child comfortable by making his environment pleasing. Keep the room temperature low, add moisture if the house is dry, and keep him in loose, comfortable clothing. Other comfort measures include the following:

- Use acetominophen as advised by your pediatrician. Reserve doses before bed to aid sleep.
- Ambient fluid from a humidifier may help. Use a cool-mist humidifier. It is just as effective as a hot-water vaporizer and safer if knocked over.
- A tepid sponge can be very soothing. Do not use alcohol or an ice bath to treat a fever. These methods can cause the blood vessels next to the skin to narrow, actually hampering the cooling process.
- Expose skin to the air. Let your child rest without blankets or sleep in just underwear or a diaper.
- However if your child feels chilled despite having a fever, cover her until she feels comfortable again.
- Do not overbundle an infant.

R E C I P E S

FROZEN FRUIT BARS

YIELD: 2 BARS

These fruit bars are superior to store-bought versions because they carry wholesome ingredients. Keep a supply in the freezer.

To make the fruit bars:
1. Mix the combinations suggested below and pour into ice pop molds (available at most supermarkets) or into small paper cups.
2. Freeze for 2 hours. Halfway through the freezing time, insert a stick, to be used as a handle.

RASPBERRY YOGURT BARS

> *5 tbsp. raspberry syrup*
> *²/₃ cup strawberry yogurt*

SUNNY CITRUS BARS

> *¹/₂ cup orange juice*
> *²/₃ cup drained crushed pineapple*

FRUITY FREEZE

> *1 jar puréed baby fruit*
> *Apple juice or white grape juice (enough to fill an empty baby food fruit jar half full)*
> *1 tbsp. granulated sugar*

BERRY ICY

Food does not have to complicated to win over a child. My mother served this sauce to dress up an angel or sponge cake. When my girls were sick, I tried the sauce over ice and my kids loved it. It's a great way to give your child essential fluids when she's ill.

> *1 8-oz. container frozen raspberries or strawberries,*
> *with sugar added*
> *1 cup crushed ice*

To make raspberry purée:
1. Thaw the fruit.
2. Purée it in a blender and then pour it through a strainer. The sauce should be smooth—seed and pulp free.
3. Pour a few tablespoons over a dish of crushed ice and serve it like ice cream with a spoon.

❦ FLU (INFLUENZA)

The flu can start as a cold, but soon your child will experience symptoms like fever, chills, headache, cough, and a sore throat. Like a cold, the flu is caused by a virus, but the flu is almost always more severe.

Flu is highly contagious. Kids spread it to one another through sneezing and coughing. In mild cases, it lasts only 3 days, but when it is severe, it can hang on for 2 weeks. Because flu is caused by a virus, antibiotics are not effective, though they might be used to treat secondary infections, such as pneumonia or ear infections.

FLU AND THE FOOD CONNECTION

Treat flu based on the symptoms it causes. A fever calls for a steady offering of liquids; if diarrhea or vomiting is present, the need for fluids will be even greater. Most flu cases present as respiratory problems, but gastrointestinal complications, including nausea, diarrhea, and vomiting, can be present, too. These symptoms will make your child's appetite plunge. Simple bland, liquid foods will be tolerated best. When feeding your child during a flu bout:

- Offer fluids as tolerated.
- If vomiting has occurred, offer only clear liquids.
- If nausea is a problem, serve bland, colorless food. Items like white rice, plain mashed or boiled potato, plain noodles, cottage cheese, plain yogurt, and vanilla ice cream are not stimulating to the senses and may be better tolerated.
- High-fat foods may be more difficult to digest. A temporary switch to lower fat foods, such as nonfat dairy products, may be easier on the tummy. Avoid high-fat snack foods such as chips, buttered popcorn, and chocolates.

- Serve small, light meals.
- Treat a sore throat or cough with warm, soothing liquids.

HOME COMFORT AND MANAGEMENT TIPS

The worst part of flu can be the headache, chills, and muscle aches that come with it. The experts say these symptoms are actually the body's way of forcing us to lie down and get some rest. Make sure your child does just that. Other ways to ease your child's discomfort and speed her recovery include the following:

- Rest is important. Your child can be in bed or on the couch, but ideally, she should be in a warm, comfortable spot.
- One of the best treatments for the aches that go with flu is a comforting massage.
- If the air in your home is very dry, use a cool-mist humidifier.
- Give lots of special attention.
- If symptoms persist for more than a week, contact your pediatrician.

RECIPES

CREAM-OF-WHEAT PUDDING

YIELD: 2 SERVINGS

Cream of wheat is one of my family's traditional sick-day foods. Try this pudding when flu symptoms subside and appetite returns. It looks like a mini soufflé when it first comes out of the oven. It tastes good when topped with a bit of whipped cream, sweet syrup, or cooked fruit. Try the Raspberry Purée on page 137 or the Chunky Applesauce on page 250.

> *1 cup scalded milk*
> *2 tbsp. cream of wheat*
> *1 tsp. butter*
> *4 tbsp. sugar*
> *2 eggs, yolks and whites separated*
> *1/4 tsp. vanilla*

1. Preheat the oven to 350°F.
2. Pour cream of wheat into scalded milk. Add butter and sugar and cook on low heat in a saucepan for 5 minutes. Set aside and allow to cool.
3. Beat egg whites until stiff and set aside.
4. Beat egg yolks into the slightly cooled cream-of-wheat mixture. Fold in egg whites and vanilla. Pour mixture into 2 1-cup-capacity custard cups that have been lightly oiled.
5. Bake for 15 minutes. Serve right away while warm.

ABC SOUP

YIELD: 2 CUPS

This soup is splendid when served with a crisp saltine or Milk Lunch cracker. Your child will no doubt spend time looking for his own initials.

> **2 cups chicken broth**
> **1 medium carrot, peeled and cut into thin slivers**
> **³/₄ cup cooked tiny alphabet egg noodles**

1. Heat the broth in a pot and add the prepared carrots. Cook for 8 minutes, or until the carrots are tender.
2. Stir in the cooked alphabet noodles and simmer for 3 to 5 minutes. Serve warm.

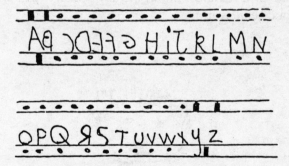

LACE SOUP

YIELD: 2 CUPS

This simple, easy-to-prepare soup will taste good to your child and be very digestible, too. It is made with only the white of the egg, so the soup is very low in fat, a desirable quality when a tummy is irritable from the flu. As the egg whites cook in the broth, they form thin white strands that resemble lace.

> *2 cups prepared chicken broth*
> *3 egg whites*
> *1 tbsp. water*
> *1 tsp. soy sauce (optional)*

1. Heat the broth until boiling, then reduce the heat to low.
2. In a bowl, mix the egg whites and the water. The egg whites should be liquidy but not frothy.
3. Stir the broth and slowly drizzle in the egg whites, stirring constantly. Try to make thin, wispy strands, not globs.
4. Cook for 3 minutes. Stir in the soy sauce, if you are using it, and serve warm.

⟶ FOOD ALLERGY

Four to 8 percent of infants and children have food allergies. Children are not born with a food allergy; they are born with the *potential* to become allergic. Theoretically, kids could be allergic to most any food, but eggs, cow's milk, peanuts, wheat, and soy protein are the most likely offenders. Cow's milk is the most common food allergen: 2 percent of infants will have an adverse reaction to cow's milk protein.

A food allergy develops when a particular food is eaten and the immune system creates an antibody to the protein in the food. Protein causes the allergic reaction. People in different countries have different food allergies, based on the source of protein in their diet. In the United States, cow's milk allergy is prevalent because of all the dairy products we consume. In Japan, soy is the most common food allergen, and in Scandinavian countries, fish is. This is a clear demonstration that frequency and volume of food ingestion can influence food allergy.

Symptoms of food allergy can occur within minutes to an hour of eating a trigger food. Food allergy symptoms can include swelling of the lips and mouth, hives, rash, wheezing, vomiting, stuffy nose, abdominal pain, and diarrhea. In severe cases, an allergy can be the cause of life-threatening anaphylactic shock.

In most children, food allergies will spontaneously resolve by the time children are 3 or 4 years old. The skin rashes that can accompany the introduction to new foods is almost always self-limiting, but a severe allergic response that includes respiratory symptoms is not likely to resolve itself with age. Children allergic to peanuts, nuts, fish, or seafood often have a lifelong allergy to these foods.

Not all food reactions are true food allergies. One third of American parents report that their infants have a rash or gastrointestinal problems associated with diet, but these are not all allergies. Many such problems are temporary food intolerances that often disappear with age. For example, oranges and tomatoes are often cited as the cause of skin irritations, but this is because the acid irritates the skin, not because the body is allergic to it. Fruit juice, because of its high sugar content, can cause loose stools. A full 20 to 30 percent of infants will develop colic regardless of the type of feeding they receive. It is important to distinguish between true food allergy and food reactions so that treatment is appropriate and so that elimination of favorite and nutritious foods is not done needlessly.

If you suspect your child has a food allergy, try to identify it. Pay attention to the onset and duration of symptoms and the type of food consumed. Keep a record of its frequency, noting the circumstances of the reaction. The only way to positively identify an allergen is to "challenge" a child's system with the suspected food and observe what happens. Such food challenges must be conducted under the supervised care of someone experienced with treating the potentially serious side effects, which include anaphylactic shock. Allergy tests, such as the IgE (immunoglobulin E) antibody test, can be useful, but their results are not always definitive. They can help narrow the field of allergenic foods, and they can be useful in identifying the foods that the child is not allergic to. IgG (immunoglobulin G) antibody, sublingual, and leukocytoxic testing have not been shown to be of any value. Contact a board-certified allergist to diagnose and treat your child's allergy. Tests may not be needed when the symptoms can be clearly linked to a particular food. The good news is that most people are allergic to only a few foods, not lots of different items.

For children who are at risk of an anaphylactic reaction, the physician will prescribe and instruct parents on the use of epinephrine injections to be used at the first sign of distress. Children who have asthma are not at an increased

FOOD ALLERGY SYMPTOMS

The following symptoms do not always indicate a food allergy, but if they persist, discuss them with your pediatrician:

- A cold that runs from April to October with a clear, runny discharge; stuffy nose, itchy nose; horizontal crease across the top of the nose caused by constant rubbing; mouth breathing
- Your infant pulls her legs up to her tummy and seems to cry in pain from cramps; chronic diarrhea; excessive gassiness and spitting up
- Dry, itchy patches of skin on the cheeks and creases of arms and legs; red, hot cheeks and a rash on the stomach that will not clear up
- Wheezing or a persistent dry cough

risk for food allergy, but if they do have a food allergy, the asthma can increase the risk of more serious side effects.

Malnutrition can be a side effect of food allergy. Fear of food reaction—on the part of both child and parent—can result in the child's undereating. Malabsorption of nutrients due to diarrhea is a potential problem, too. At least one case of rickets in a 4-year-old child on a milk-free diet to treat milk allergy has been reported. Long-term elimination of such major items in the basic food groups as wheat, milk, or eggs require that the nutrients contained in these food groups be replaced by other nonallergenic foods rich in the missing nutrients.

FOOD ALLERGIES AND THE FOOD CONNECTION

In a family in which food allergies are common, a mother's diet while pregnant and breast-feeding may be the place to start prevention. The results of one often-cited 1991 study conducted by Rundit Chandra, M.D., found when mothers eliminated the following foods while pregnant and lactating, the incidence of allergy-related eczema was reduced in their children: chicken eggs, fish, peanuts, and cow's milk. In another promising study, published in 1993 in the Annals of Allergy, mothers avoided ingesting milk, eggs, tomato, fish, shellfish, and nuts during lactation and used soy formula for supplementation when needed. They also carefully introduced solid foods when their babies were 8 months, not 4 or 6 months old. A restricted menu for pregnant and lactating mothers for the prevention of allergies is not an across-the-board recommendation for new mothers. The diet can be difficult to follow, and though results of the studies are promising, the diet does not guarantee allergy prevention.

To prevent or reduce the risk of food allergy when there is a prominent component of your family's genetic make-up:

■ Exclusively breast-feed your baby for the first 6 months. Once you introduce solids, continue to breast-feed as long as possible for the immunities it confers.

■ Delay introducing solids until your baby is 6 months old. Introduce new foods singly.

■ Start with iron-fortified rice cereal, since rice is rarely a cause of food allergy.

■ Wheat and egg whites are common allergens. Hold off introducing them until your child is 1 year old.

■ If a food appears to cause an allergic reaction, do not try serving the food again for 3 months.

■ Establish a tolerance level if possible. Small, infrequent servings of an allergenic food may be tolerated.

■ Cooking can sometimes make the allergenic foods tolerable. This is particularly true for apples, potatoes, and carrots. Cow's milk, egg whites, peanuts, soybeans, shrimp, and codfish will not be made nonallergenic by cooking.

■ Since it is the protein part of a food that is the problem, nonprotein forms of the food, such as peanut oil instead of whole peanuts, may be tolerated.

■ If a food is associated with a severe reaction that effects breathing, reintroduce that food only under a physician's care. Uncontrolled, unsupervised food challenges at home can be dangerous.

Once a food allergy develops, treat it by avoidance of the food. See pages 151–54 for shopping considerations for special diets.

COW'S MILK ALLERGY

Cow's milk allergy is not synonymous with lactose intolerance. *Cow's milk allergy* means your child is allergic to the protein in the milk. *Lactose intolerance* refers to the sugar known as lactose. Read more about lactose intolerance on page 182. If your child is allergic to cow's milk, you should be aware of the following:

■ Infants who develop cow's milk allergy should not be given other common allergenic foods such as eggs, chocolate, peanuts, fish, and citrus.

■ Infants allergic to cow's milk may also become allergic to soy milk, so a casein or lactalbumin whey formula may be advised. Ask your pediatrician.

■ Neither goat's nor sheep's milk should be given to infants. They are not adequate sources of vitamin D, iron, or folic acid.

■ Older children can try pasteurized sheep's milk and goat's milk, but be alert to allergy symptoms. Kids can be allergic to the protein in these milks, too. They do contain lactose and thus are not appropriate for children with a lactose intolerance.

■ If a milk-free diet is required children need alternate sources of calcium and vitamin D. Children 1 year and older require 800 milligrams of calcium and 10 micrograms of vitamin D daily. Calcium can be obtained in orange juice fortified with calcium. Good vitamin D sources include fish, liver, salmon, sardines, mackerel, and egg yolk.

GLUTEN ALLERGY (CELIAC DISEASE)

Celiac disease is an inherited condition and the most common intestinal disorder causing malnutrition in children. Children are sensitive to gliadin, a protein found in wheat, rye, barley, and oats. Symptoms include failure to gain weight, weight loss, and soft, frequent, bulky stools. If your child has a gluten allergy:

■ Avoid all gluten.
■ Your child can have cornmeal, cornstarch, and flour made from soybean, garbanzo beans, potato, arrowroot, and rice.
■ It may be necessary to place your child on a short-term lactose-free diet if the gluten allergy has caused a secondary lactose intolerance.

WHEAT ALLERGY

Children can be sensitive to wheat but not specifically to the gluten. If this is the case with your child:

■ Include nonwheat flour—from rye, oats, and barley—in his diet.
■ Be aware that wheat is a common thickener and additive to many processed foods.

EGG ALLERGY

It is usually the egg white that causes egg allergies. Egg protein can be found in unexpected sources, such as the foaming agent in root beer.

CORN ALLERGY

If your child is highly sensitive to corn, it may be necessary to avoid even corn oil and corn syrup, which contain traces of corn protein. Most commercially prepared candies and desserts contain some form of corn. Corn, as cornstarch, is used in numerous paper products to prevent sticking and is even used in the glue on stamps. Avoid such obvious sources of corn as popcorn and cooked corn.

SOY ALLERGY

If your child has a soy allergy, be aware that soy takes many forms. Hydrolyzed vegetable protein or textured vegetable protein are often made with soy products. Tofu, a popular ingredient in Chinese food, will need to be avoided. Non-dairy creamers may be made with soy, and soy may be used as a filler in cold cuts, sausage, and in cheese substitutes.

PEANUT ALLERGY

Peanut allergy is often a lifetime problem capable of causing serious reactions. Parents will need to be ever vigilant if this allergy is present.

- Peanuts are added to baked goods and snack foods to boost protein.
- Avoid all sources of peanuts, including peanut butter and peanut hull flour.
- Nutritional supplements may have peanuts as the source of protein.
- Highly sensitive children may need to avoid peanut oil.

FISH OR SHELLFISH ALLERGY

Seafood reactions often occur suddenly, and they can be severe. Even seafood odors and skin contact can elicit a reaction in highly sensitive children. All fish and fish products must be avoided. Results from a 1992 study published in the Journal of Allergy and Clinical Immunology showed that fresh tuna and fresh salmon caused a reaction, but the canned versions did not; it is possible that the high temperatures in canning make the allergens unstable. Because fish allergies have the potential to be very dangerous, do not experiment with tolerance levels except under the supervision of an allergist.

HOME MANAGEMENT AND COMFORT TIPS

Plan for accidents and be glad when they don't happen. Discuss with your doctor the need for your child to wear a Medic Alert bracelet or necklace. If epinephrine is needed, make sure that all your child's caregivers know about its use. Treat your child like any other child and treat food allergies in a matter-of-fact way. He needs to be informed and responsible about preventing food allergies. Allergy coping strategies include the following:

▪ When your child is invited to a party, let the hostess know about the allergy when you RSVP. Volunteer to drop off an allergy-free treat before the party if necessary.
▪ Try to avoid making a big fuss in front of other children.
▪ When traveling, pack food or at least carry a supply of ready-to-eat snacks you can count on.
▪ Shop wisely (see pages 151–54).
▪ Involve your child and the whole family in preventing allergic reactions.
▪ Talk to your child's teacher and homeroom parent about your child's food allergy.
▪ Ask the pediatrician about the use of antihistamines to treat itching.
▪ Contact the Food Allergy Network listed in the box on page 155.

WHAT TO LOOK FOR AT THE SUPERMARKET WHEN YOUR CHILD HAS A FOOD ALLERGY

Source and Foods that May Need to Be Omitted	How It May Be Listed on the Label	Ingredient Substitutes or Alternative Foods of Comparative Nutritional Value
MILK Fluid milk, buttermilk, evaporated milk, cream, nonfat dry milk, condensed milk, all cheeses, yogurt, butter, many margarines, egg nog, ice cream, sherbet, egg substitutes like Egg Beaters, most nondairy creamers and whipped toppings, macaroni and cheese, creamed soups and sauces, pancakes, waffles, coffee cakes and breads, chocolate candies, fudge, instant potatoes, cookies, custards, puddings, many breads and many crackers, hot cocoa mixes, breakfast beverage mixes, luncheon meats, sausage	Instant nonfat dry milk, nonfat milk, milk solids, whey, curds, casein, casein hydrolysate, sodium caseinate, calcium caseinate, lactalbumin, lactoglobulin, cheese, cheese food, butter, buttermilk, cottage cheese, custard, milk chocolate, sour cream, Simplesse (fat substitute containing milk protein)	• Milk protein hydrolyzed formulas, soy milk, and soy milk formulas • Water or juice in baked goods, milk-free margarines, nondairy creamers without milk protein • Meats labeled kosher and products labeled "parve" do not contain milk products • Moderate calcium sources include fortified tofu or soybean curd; calcium-fortified orange juice; dark green leafy vegetables like kale, broccoli, and collards; dry beans; canned fish with bones; soup and stews cooked with bones
LACTOSE Milk, cheese, cottage cheese, sour cream, ice cream, sherbet, pudding, some acidophilus milks, buttermilk, sweetened condensed milk, evaporated milk, yogurt, instant potatoes, butter, margarines containing milk solids, powdered eggs, baby food dinners and desserts, gravies, salad dressings, whipped toppings, breakfast drinks, instant cocoa mixes, powdered soft drinks, antacids, birth-control pills, buttered popcorn, creamed soups, powdered coffee creamers, some vitamin supplements (read labels), asthma medications, lunch meats/cold cuts (except kosher), hot dogs, sausages	Milk, lactose, whey, curds, milk byproducts, milk solids, dry milk solids, nonfat dry milk powder	• Lactose-reduced milks (Lactaid), low-lactose dairy products, milklike beverages (Vitamite) • Liquid and tablet lactase enzymes (Dairy Ease, Lactrase, Lactaid, Lactogest) added to lactose-containing foods or taken before eating • Hard cheeses and yogurt with active cultures contain lactose, but may be fairly well tolerated • Alternative calcium sources include soybean milk products and tofu (if processed and/or fortified with calcium), dark green leafy vegetables, dry beans, and fish with tiny bones

Source and Foods that May Need to Be Omitted	How It May Be Listed on the Label	Ingredient Substitutes or Alternative Foods of Comparative Nutritional Value

WHEAT/GLUTEN
 	
Breads, cakes, cookies, pasta, macaroni, spaghetti, noodles, soup, most crackers, doughnuts, pancakes, biscuits, waffles, ready-to-eat and cooked cereals containing wheat, wheat breaded mixes, corn meal mix, salad dressings, gravies, ice cream cones, malted beverages, Postum, cracked wheat, bulgur, rice pilaf, couscous, tabouleh, whiskey, vodka, ale, beer, gin, some wines, some canned peas, beans and corn, soy sauce, instant puddings, some nondairy creamers
	Flour, all-purpose flour, wheat flour, gluten, wheat, cake flour, whole-wheat flour, graham flour, farina, wheat starch, wheat germ, wheat bran, bran, phosphated wheat, semolina, sodium glutenate, MSG (monosodium glutenate), food starch, vegetable starch, vegetable gum, modified food starch	**Okay for wheat free but not gluten free:**
		Rye flour, oat four, oatmeal, barley, amaranth, buckwheat, triticale
		Okay for wheat and gluten free:
		Potatoes, potato flour, rice, rice flour, whole-grain rice wafers, corn flour, corn tortillas, cornmeal, cereals made with corn or rice, bean thread noodles, soy flour, millet, arrowroot, tapioca, pasta made from allowed flours
		
		• Substitute for 1 cup wheat flour for use in baking:
		
		  1 cup purified wheat starch
		  3/4 cup potato meal
		  7/8 cup rich flour
		  1/2 cup potato starch flour plus 1/2 cup rye or soy flour
		  1 cup corn flour
		  1 scant cup cornmeal (fine)
		  3/4 cup cornmeal (coarse)
		  1/2 cup barley flour
		  1 1/3 cups oat flakes
		  1 cup rye flour or meal
		
		• Substitute for 1 tbsp. wheat flour for use in thickening sauces, gravies, and puddings:
		
		  1/2 tbsp. cornstarch
		  1 tbsp. waxy rice or cornstarch
		  1/2 tbsp. potato-starch flour
		  1/2 tbsp. rice starch
		  1/2 tbsp. arrowroot starch
		  1 tbsp. quick-cooking tapioca
		  2 tbsp. granular cereal
		  1 whole egg, 2 egg whites, or 2 egg yolks

EGG

All forms of eggs; French toast; fritters; cakes; cookies; cake doughnuts; pastries; muffins; soufflés; mayonnaise; Hollandaise sauce; some salad dressings; marshmallows; candies such as chocolate, fondants, and divinity; eggnog; egg breads and rolls; sweet rolls glazed with egg; noodle soups; meat loaf, casseroles; custard; cream pies; pumpkin pies; most egg substitutes; French-style ice creams; other ice creams; sherbets; breaded foods; pretzels; pasta made with eggs; instant breakfast beverages; meringues; root beer; some coffees and wines (clarifying agent); Simplesse (fat substitute)

Eggs, egg powder, dried egg, albumin, egg yolk, egg white, dried egg white, dried egg solids, egg solids, egg yolks, globulin, vitellin, ovovitellin, ovomucin, ovomucoid

- Egg-free egg substitutes (check labels)
- In baking, replace 1 egg with: ½ tsp. baking powder + 2 tbsp. flour + 2 tbsp. liquid; or gelatin mixture: soften 1 tbsp. unflavored gelatin in 3 tbsp. cold water; add 3 tbsp. boiling water; cool and beat until frothy; add to recipe (reduce other liquid by 2 tbsp.)
- Alternate foods include ready-to-eat or hot breakfast cereals, baking powder biscuits, egg-free breads, cornstarch puddings, spaghetti noodles and macaroni, fruit pies

CORN

Very widely used in food processing. Fresh, frozen, or canned corn or mixed vegetables, vegetable soups, cornmeal, cornbread, corn tortillas, grits, hominy, masa harina, corn flakes and other breakfast cereals, popcorn, cornstarch in puddings, sauces, and pie fillings, corn oil for cooking, margarines and salad dressings, corn sweetener, Karo syrup or confectioners' sugar, candy, marshmallows, jellies, gelatin desserts, soft drinks, cookies, ice cream, sherbet, most baking powders, fermented beverages made with corn (like bourbon, vodka, gin, whiskey, and beer), snacks like corn chips, vinegar, bread coating on fish sticks and on pans to keep French bread from sticking, as filler in vitamin capsules

Corn, corn syrup, corn meal, corn flour, masa harina, corn starch, corn solids, corn oil, cornmeal, vegetable oil, vegetable starch, vegetable gum, food starch, hydrolyzed vegetable protein, maize, popcorn, grits, hominy, corn sweeteners (including dextrose, dextrin, ceruloce, buretose, glucose, sorbitol, and HFCS, or high-fructose corn syrup)

- White, whole wheat, or rye bread or pancakes; wheat-flour tortillas
- Wheat, rice, or oatmeal cereals
- Safflower or soybean oils and margarines
- Jamaican rum (must be made from cane sugar)
- Granulated cane or beet sugar, honey, pure maple syrup
- Wheat, potato, or rice flour as thickeners
- Baking soda and cream of tartar (for leavening agent)

Source and Foods that May Need to Be Omitted	How It May Be Listed on the Label	Ingredient Substitutes or Alternative Foods of Comparative Nutritional Value
SOY Tofu or soybean curd, vegetable protein in casserole mixes and meat extenders, veggieburgers, luncheon meats, bacon bits, meats or fish canned in oil, canned soups, high-protein breads and cereals, many margarines and salad dressings, fried foods in restaurants, fast-food shakes, cheese substitutes, soy sauce, Teriyaki sauce, Worcestershire sauce, soy nuts, soy infant formulas, soy milk, miso, tempeh, soy oil	Soy, soy flour, soya flour, lecithin (emulsifier), vegetable protein, TVP (textured vegetable protein), soy protein, soy concentration, soy protein isolate, soy granules, vegetable starch, hydrolyzed vegetable protein, vegetable gum, soy oil, soybean oil, vegetable oil, soy milk	• Corn or safflower oils and margarines, butter • All fresh or plain meats • Homemade casseroles, fish canned in water • Corn and rice cereals
SULFITES Dried fruits and vegetables (especially light colored), fruit juices, some salad bar contents, shellfish, fruits, instant potatoes, potato mixes, avocado dips, honey, wine, beer, prescription drugs	Sulfur dioxide (SO_2), potassium sulfite (K_2SO_3), sodium sulfite (Na_2SO_3), potassium metabisulfite ($K_2S_2O_5$), potassium bisulfite ($KHSO_3$), sodium metabisulfite ($Na_2S_2O_5$), sodium bisulfite ($NaHSO_3$), sulfiting agent, sulfiting agents, vegetable fresheners	• Alternative antibrowning agents such as citric acid, tartaric acid, ascorbic acid, erythorbic acid • Sulfite-free wine products • Baked potatoes

Reprinted with permission from Kendall, P.A. "Managing Food Allergies and Sensitivities." *Topics of Clinical Nutrition:* 9:(3) 1–10, 1994.

HELP! WHAT CAN I FEED MY CHILD?

The only good news about a food allergy is that your family is not the first to face the problem. For help, start at your local library. You will find, next to the traditional cookbooks, an assortment of specialty allergy cookbooks, many of them excellent, most of them written by parents in response to their own child's need for specialty foods. Another good option is to contact one of the organizations or food companies listed below.

Organizations and Newsletters

> Allergy Education Service
> 1202-1175 Broadview Avenue
> Toronto, Ontario
> Canada M4K 2F9
> (416) 425-7072
>
> Asthma and Allergy Foundation of America
> 1125 15th Street NW, Suite 502
> Washington, D.C. 20005
> (800) 727-8462
>
> Celiac Sprue Association/United States of America, Inc.
> P.O. Box 31700
> Omaha, NE 68131-0700
> (402) 558-0600
>
> The Food Allergy Network
> Anne Munoz-Furlong
> 4744 Holly Avenue
> Fairfax, VA 22030
> (800) 929-4040
>
> *Newsletter for People with Lactose Intolerance and Milk Allergy*
> Jane Zukin Commercial Writing Service
> P.O. Box 3074
> Iowa City, IA 52244

Rodale's Allergy Relief Newsletter
33 E Minor Street
Emmaus, PA 18049

Specialty Food Companies

Dietary Specialties Inc.
P.O. Box 227
Rochester, NY 14601
(716) 263-2787

Ener G Food Inc.
P.O. Box 84487
Seattle, WA 98124
(800) 331-5222

Kingsmill Diet Foods
1399 Kennedy Road, Unit 17
Scarborough, Ontario
Canada MIP 2L6
(416) 755-1124

Shiloh Farms
P.O. Box 97
Sulphur Springs, AR 72786
(501) 298-3297

Wholesome and Hearty Foods
2422 SE Hawthorne Boulevard
Portland, OR 97214

Worthington Foods
Soyamel Facts and Recipes (lactose free)
Worthington, OH 43085
(614) 885-9511

RECIPES

BLUEBERRY MUFFINS—HOLD THE WHEAT!

YIELD: 1 DOZEN MUFFINS

Rice flour is available at specialty stores and health food stores. This recipe, along with those for Oatmeal Rice Cookies and Hearty Oatmeal Bread, which follow, were adapted with permission from "The Food Sensitivity: A Resource Including Recipes, in Food Sensitivity Series, from the American Dietetic Association, Chicago, Illinois, 1985.

> *2 cups rice flour*
> *4 tsp. baking powder*
> *¹/₂ cup brown sugar*
> *1 tsp. salt*
> *2 medium eggs*
> *1 ¹/₄ cups milk*
> *3 tbsp. butter, melted*
> *1 tsp. vanilla extract*
> *1 ¹/₂ cups fresh or frozen blueberries*

1. Preheat the oven to 375°F.
2. Sift the dry ingredients together.
3. Beat the eggs with the milk, butter, and vanilla.
4. Add the flour mixture to the eggs; stir gently until all the dry ingredients are moistened, but do not overbeat.
5. With a wooden spoon, fold in the blueberries. Do not over-mix, or the batter will turn blue.
6. Fill lightly oiled muffin tins and bake for 18 minutes or until brown.

OATMEAL RICE COOKIES (EGG, WHEAT, AND MILK FREE!)

YIELD: 18 COOKIES

> *2 sticks milk-free margarine*
> *1 cup brown sugar*
> *1 cup granulated sugar*
> *1 tsp. vanilla extract*
> *1 cup rice flour*
> *1 tsp. salt*
> *4 tsp. baking powder*
> *³/₄ cup water*
> *3 cups oatmeal*
> *¹/₂ cup chopped nuts or raisins*

1. Preheat the oven to 350°F.
2. Cream the margarine with the sugars and vanilla.
3. Sift together the flour, salt, and baking powder.
4. Add the flour mixture alternately with the water, until all ingredients are well combined.
5. Stir in the nuts or raisins.
6. Drop by spoonfuls onto a lightly greased baking sheet and cook for 10 minutes or until lightly browned.

HEARTY OATMEAL BREAD
(NO MILK, NO EGG)

YIELD: 2 LOAVES

2 cups oatmeal
2¹/₂ cups very hot water
¹/₂ cup molasses
1 tbsp. salt
¹/₄ cup salad oil
6–7 cups of flour
2 packages yeast

1. Pour 2 cups of the hot water over the oatmeal and set aside.
2. In a separate bowl, sprinkle the yeast over the remaining ¹/₂ cup of hot water and stir in 1 tbsp. of the molasses. Cover with a paper towel and let "proof" for 5 minutes. After 5 minutes, the yeast and water mixture should have formed a soft, foamy mass—proof that the yeast is active.
3. Combine the yeast with the oatmeal, the remaining molasses, and the salt and salad oil. Stir in 1 cup of the flour, then add enough of the remaining flour, 1 cup at a time, until the dough can hold its shape but is not crumbly or too dry.
4. On a floured board, knead the dough for 5 minutes until it is smooth and elastic. Return dough to a greased bowl and set it in a draft-free spot to rise for 1 hour.
5. Punch down the dough and divide it in half. Shape it into balls and place them in 2 lightly greased bread pans, each 9" × 5". Let the dough rise for 1 hour or until doubled in size.
6. Preheat the oven to 350°F. Bake 30 minutes or until the bread sounds hollow when tapped. Remove bread from the pans and let it cool before slicing it.

⌇⌇ HEADACHE

Headache is a common complaint of childhood, and by age 7, 40 percent of children will have experienced a headache, which they usually described as pressure or an aching pain in the head. The causes of headache are numerous and can include dental problems, fever, sinus infection, fatigue, and injury. Poor vision, though often accused, is rarely the cause of a headache. When stress, worry, or muscle contraction cause headache, it is usually described as a pain in the back of the head.

Rest almost always alleviates a headache, and in most cases, they are only a temporary annoyance. A persistent headache that limits activity or is linked with vomiting or an injury or that affects vision requires further investigation, including a neurological examination and a blood pressure check.

Migraine headaches, caused by a constriction of blood vessels that diminishes blood flow to the areas in the brain, occurs in 5 percent of children. Migraine often runs in families and may be associated with nausea, loss of appetite, pallor, irritability, and light sensitivity.

HEADACHES AND THE FOOD CONNECTION

A few dietary factors can aid in the relief and prevention of headaches. Some children experience headache when they are hungry, so regular meals and nutritional snacks are a must. The abrupt elimination of caffeine can cause intense but temporary headaches in children who consume a lot of caffeine, mostly from soda and some candy. Ice cream, because it is so cold, is a common cause of headache. Chocolate, ripe cheese, and freshly baked yeast products contain tyramine. Tyramine is a naturally occurring chemical that can, in susceptible individuals, cause cerebral blood vessels to dilate, resulting in a headache. Monosodium glutamate

(MSG) can cause headaches in sensitive individuals. MSG sensitivity is often referred to as Chinese restaurant syndrome. It is not common; when it does occur, it is usually heralded by a tightness in the chest and a burning sensation in the back of the neck and not just headache alone.

To ease a headache:

- Offer light food; don't force food.
- Try offering cool foods, such as sliced fruit; avoid very hot foods, such as soup or stew, or very cold foods, such as ice cream or ice pops.
- Look at the family meal schedule and snack routine. If headaches occur at a predictable time, try a light snack or meal every 2 to 3 hours to see if it has any effect.
- Some migraine sufferers can identify trigger foods. Common suspects include chocolate, cheese, and nitrite-containing foods (nitrites are found in processed meats). A diary may help identify trigger foods.
- Stop gum chewing. Excessive gum chewing can cause a headache.

HOME COMFORT AND MANAGEMENT TIPS

Rest, in an environment with little stimulation, can help ease your child's headache. Keep the lights low and the temperature comfortable. The following can make your child more comfortable, too:

- Try a cool compress on the head.
- A gentle neck massage can be very soothing or, at the very least, distracting.
- Gently massage your child's temples.
- Help your child try the relaxation techniques on pages 266–68.
- A hot shower or warm bath can relieve some headaches.
- Biofeedback therapy has been helpful in the treatment of migraine headaches. It must be conducted by a therapist

trained in biofeedback techniques. Ask your pediatrician for a referral.

▪ Keep a diary of headache occurrences. Is there a pattern to the headaches? Are they associated with an activity? Do they occur at a particular time of day? You may be able to identify a pattern and then experiment with ways to prevent further headaches.

▪ Occasionally, fumes or strong odors can be the cause of headaches. Don't let your child play with perfume and don't use cleaners or air fresheners with strong household fragrances when your child has a headache. Be aware that monoxide poisoning, which can be caused by poorly vented heating systems, can first appear as a headache.

▪ Do not let recurrent headaches go unexplored.

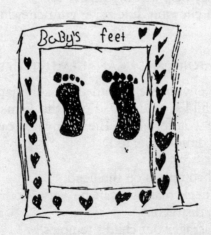

RECIPES

APPLE TART

YIELD: 1 10-INCH TART

The goodness of this simple tart might be able to distract your child from an aching head. Serve it at room temperature, perhaps with a dab of sweet whipped cream.

For the crust:
1 ½ cups all-purpose flour
5 tbsp. cold butter, cut into small chunks
¼ cup granulated sugar
1 egg yolk

For the filling:
6 apples, peeled, cored, and cut into slices
1 tbsp. water
¼ cup apricot or seedless raspberry jam

To make the crust:
1. In a bowl, combine the flour and the butter, using clean fingers. Blend the two ingredients together until the butter pieces are no bigger than a grain of rice and the dough is mealy.
2. With a wooden spoon, blend in the egg yolk and sugar.
3. Shape the dough into a ball and refrigerate 5 minutes.

To make the filling:
4. While the dough is in the refrigerator, combine the apples with 1 tbsp. of water.
5. Cover them and cook in the microwave on high heat for 3 minutes. Set aside until ready to use.

To complete the tart:

6. Preheat the oven to 350°F.
7. On a floured board, roll the cold pastry into a 10-in. circle.
8. Place the pastry in a pie plate or tart pan. Prick holes in the bottom of the crust.
9. Bake the crust for 5 minutes, then remove it from the oven and set it aside.
10. Drain the juice from the apples and mix it with the jam. Arrange the apples in a spiral over the cooked crust. Drizzle the jam and juice mixture over the apples.
11. Bake the tart for 30 minutes. Allow it to cool to room temperature before serving.

SPAGHETTI WITH PEANUT SAUCE

YIELD: 2–3 SERVINGS

This good sauce for pasta is an adaptation of one used to flavor Thai food. I leave out the traditional spicy red pepper flakes since my kids don't like them. Cream of coconut is so expensive that it is optional in this dish. When I have it on hand, I use it; the results are creamier, but even without it, my daughter Sarah loves spaghetti with peanut sauce.

> 1 1/2 cups chicken broth
> 1 clove garlic, finely minced
> 5 tbsp. creamy or chunky peanut butter
> 1/4 cup cream of coconut (optional)
> 1 tbsp. soy sauce
> 1 tbsp. cornstarch
> 1 tbsp. brown sugar
> 8 oz. spaghetti, cooked
> 1/4 cup chopped peanuts for garnish
> 1/4 cup fresh red pepper, chopped, for garnish (optional)

1. In a small saucepan, sauté the garlic in 2 tbsp. of the chicken broth for 2 minutes.
2. Add the remaining chicken broth, peanut butter, and cream of coconut, stirring until the peanut butter is liquified.
3. Add the cornstarch, soy sauce, and brown sugar. Mix with a spoon and break up any lumps.
4. Cook the sauce until it thickens a bit more (about 3 to 4 minutes).
5. Pour the sauce over the pasta. Toss until well combined. Sprinkle with the garnish and serve at room temperature.

CULTURED QUICHE

YIELD: 1 PIE

A warm piece of quiche, a few slices of summertime tomatoes, and a glass of cool milk makes a lovely lunch. Substitute melon or orange slices for the tomatoes and you now have a yummy breakfast. The yogurt in this recipe blends well with the cheese flavor. Always serve quiche after it cools to room temperature, as it tastes best that way—plus, eager little mouths can get burned by the hot cheese.

1 prepared single crust
3 large eggs
1 cup plain yogurt
1 cup grated cheddar, Swiss, or Muenster cheese
Pinch of fresh nutmeg
1 lb. cooked and drained or frozen and thawed chopped spinach
(optional)

1. Preheat the oven to 350°F.
2. Combine all the ingredients except the spinach. Mix well.
3. Fold in the spinach and pour the whole mixture into the pie crust.
4. Bake for 45 minutes or until done. Insert a knife into the center of the quiche; if it comes out clean, it's done. Cool to room temperature and serve warm.

HYPERACTIVITY (ATTENTION DEFICIT HYPERACTIVITY DISORDER)

The number of children with attention deficit hyperactivity disorder (ADHD) is estimated at 4 to 10 percent of American children. In general, children with ADHD have difficulty focusing on one task and paying attention and are more physically active (hyperactive) as compared to their peers. Some children can have attention deficit disorder (ADD) without hyperactivity; these kids lack the ability to focus and pay attention. Both ADD and ADHD are more common among boys.

The problem is not a matter of a child's being deliberately willful or disobedient. Though the cause is not clearly understood, ADHD is believed to be due to abnormal levels of brain chemicals called neurotransmitters, specifically norepinephrine and dopamine. Children with a high number of indicative behavioral characteristics, such as the inability to stay with one task or one game, are said to have the condition. To be true indicators of ADHD, these identifying behaviors should occur in a variety of settings, including home, school, or a friend's house. It is essential to identify kids with this disorder because they often need individualized education plans to prevent poor school performance and low self-esteem.

The condition is treated with medications that include Dexedrine, Ritalin, Cylert, Norpramin. Side effects of these medications can include insomnia, loss of appetite, decrease in growth rate, and stomach pain.

ATTENTION DEFICIT HYPERACTIVITY DISORDER AND THE FOOD CONNECTION

THE FEINGOLD DIET

In 1975, Benjamin Feingold, M.D., published the book *Why Your Child Is Hyperactive*. It provided a dietary treatment for ADHD. Dr. Feingold developed the diet based on a regimen he had successfully used with treating adults who had aspirin sensitivity. He extended the program to include hyperactive children and reported the diet to be beneficial in treating ADHD. The diet advocates a menu void of all synthetic colors and flavors, some preservatives, and foods that contain salicylates, including oranges, apples, grapes, plums, cucumbers, and tomatoes. Salicylates are a naturally occurring chemical similar to aspirin that Dr. Feingold says affects behavior. Many parents give testimonials to its effectiveness, but there is little scientific evidence that supports it. The results of several double-blind controlled clinical trials do not verify the sweeping claims Dr. Feingold makes regarding the diet's effectiveness. In 1982, the National Institutes of Health's Consensus Report stated that the diet may help only a very small subgroup of patients. More recently, Esther H. Wender, M.D., reviewed the research regarding this dietary treatment and was unable to find a causal relationship between food additives and children's behavior.

Despite the lack of scientific evidence, many families swear that a change in diet affects their child's behavior. The Feingold Diet, because it is restrictive, can be difficult to follow. Parents who choose to proceed down this dietary path must not overlook the degree of stress sticking to and enforcing such a regimen can cause. In children who may already be confrontational, a request for adherence to a restrictive menu may result in more agitation. Then again, some researchers explain the reported benefits of the diet by the fact that parents create a more structured menu and pay close attention to what their child eats. The diet is not likely to cause nutritional problems. Some favorite vitamin C foods, such as oranges and tomatoes, are eliminated, but limes, lemons, and grapefruits are allowed and can provide a source of vitamin C, as can fresh vegetables. Families who want more information can contact:

The Feingold Association
127 East Main Street, Suite 106
Riverhead, NY 11901
(800) 321-3287

SUGAR AND ATTENTION DEFICIT HYPERACTIVITY DISORDER

Sugar has long been suggested as the cause of rowdy, inattentive behavior in children, but when examined scientifically, study results don't support this perception. A 1994 study published in the *New England Journal of Medicine* looked at sugar and behavior in two groups of children. One group consisted of children whose parents believed sugar effected their behavior. The other group consisted of kids with behavior described as "normal" after eating sugar. The children in both groups were fed a diet that varied in sugar content: the diet ranged from high in sugar to high in sugar substitutes, such as aspartame (Equal) or saccharine. Neither the children, parents, or researchers knew who was getting the sugar-filled or the sugar-free diet. After 3 weeks, none of the diets caused the kids to be "hyper," including the high-sugar diet. The researchers believe that it is not sugar that effects behavior but the social situation in which it is consumed. Gather a group of kids together, give them a party—with or without sugar—and they are very likely to get rambunctious. Additional research actually suggests that sugar may have a calming effect. When infants were given a few drops of sugar before immunization shots or circumcision, the babies fed the sugar cried less.

Aspartame, a popular sugar substitute, has been suggested as a cause of hyperactive behavior. However, in a 1994 study published in the journal *Pediatrics* that gave kids with ADHD aspartame in amounts 10 times normal consumption, the aspartame had no effect on their behavior.

MEGAVITAMIN THERAPY

There is no evidence that vitamin therapy can treat ADHD. Large doses of supplements can be dangerous to children. Vitamins B_6, A, and D can be toxic when consumed in amounts that far exceed the RDA.

FOOD ALLERGY

Food allergies can affect behavior, but they are not the cause of ADHD. If a food allergy is suspected, allergy testing and an elimination diet will be needed to identify it. Medical evidence identifying food allergy as a common contributor to ADHD is lacking. The stress induced by an elimination diet is not to be underestimated. Seek help from a registered dietitian with experience in food-elimination diets to avoid nutritional inadequacies. The risk of nutritional deficiencies should not be great if foods are eliminated for a short period and entire food groups are not avoided unnecessarily.

CAFFEINE

The effect caffeine has will depend on the child and the amount consumed. Caffeine is a central nervous system stimulant; consumed in excess, it can affect behavior and sleep. Observe the effect caffeine has on your child's behavior. Some kids with ADD, particularly adolescents, can actually improve their ability to focus and concentrate if they consume small amounts of caffeine before school or before homework.

FOOD RECOMMENDATIONS FOR CHILDREN WITH ATTENTION DEFICIT HYPERACTIVITY DISORDER

Many dietary approaches have been advocated for the treatment of ADHD. Though dietary treatments are claimed to be effective by some parents, the research does not verify the testimonials. For this reason, most family doctors do not include diet—besides meeting normal nutritional needs for growth and good health—as part of the treatment. Food and the environment it is served in does have a subtle effect on health, behavior, and well-being. To maximize the potential benefit food can have on behavior, consider the following strategies:

▪ Serve a breakfast that carries some protein, such as 1 egg, 2 tablespoons peanut butter, 1 ounce of cheese, 8 ounces of milk, or 1 or 2 links of sausage. Protein can improve midmorning attentiveness.
▪ Serve balanced, complete meals.
▪ Keep track of weight and height. If weight gain occurs, do not restrict food, but serve low-fat snacks and increase activity.
▪ Structure mealtimes: stick with a time schedule and a predictable table setup.
▪ Avoid meal distractions: no phone calls, no TV, no toys. Establish rules of table conversation and teach table manners, too.
▪ Be alert to the effect medication has on nutrition, specifically appetite and stomachaches. Inform the doctor of problems; a dose adjustment may be needed.

HOW THE FAMILY CAN HELP

A disruptive home, stress, or poor parental support do not cause ADHD, but they can add to behavior problems. Children with ADHD often have low self-esteem. The family can help a child find an area of competence. It could be keeping a special collection (stamps, rocks, shells), drawing, caring for a pet, or acting. Ask the teacher for advice. Learning disabilities can accompany ADHD. Develop an individualized education plan with the school.

RECIPES

BREAKFAST SOUFFLÉ

YIELD: 4 SERVINGS

Mornings are busy, so count on this easy-to-prepare, protein-rich breakfast. Put it together the night before, let it sit in the refrigerator, and pop it in the oven while coffee brews and the family gets dressed to meet the day.

> *8 slices of bread, fresh or stale (Italian works great)*
> *1 1/2 cups grated cheddar cheese*
> *1 3/4 cups milk*
> *6 large eggs*
> *Grated fresh nutmeg*

1. Lightly butter a flat 9" × 13" baking dish. Arrange the bread evenly in the dish.
2. Beat until smooth all the remaining ingredients, including a bit of the fresh nutmeg.
3. Pour the egg mixture over the bread slices, cover, and refrigerate overnight.
4. In the morning, place the dish in a cold oven turned to 375°F. Bake for 45 minutes. It will be golden and puffy. Serve right away with a large spoon.

HOT COCOA

YIELD: 1 CUP

Store-bought cocoa mixes don't have the flavor of homemade and they often don't carry as much protein. This recipe uses milk, a good protein source, and the cocoa powder carries caffeine, which may help midmorning attentiveness.

> *1 tbsp. cocoa powder*
> *1 tbsp. granulated sugar*
> *1 cup milk*

1. In a small saucepan, mix ¼ cup of the milk with the cocoa and sugar.
2. Stir on medium heat until the cocoa and sugar are well blended.
3. Stir in the remaining milk and heat for 2 or 3 minutes, but don't let it boil. Serve warm.

⤪ IRON-DEFICIENCY ANEMIA

Approximately 3 to 30 percent of children between 6 months and 3 years old develop iron-deficiency anemia. It occurs in young children when the supply of iron they are born with is used up and is not replenished. Children are at greater risk of developing iron-deficiency anemia than adults because they use a lot of iron for growth.

Iron makes up part of the hemoglobin in blood, which carries oxygen to cells. Values known as hematocrit, hemoglobin, and mean corpuscular value are used to determine red blood cell count and diagnose anemia. At your child's 1-year checkup, a routine iron blood test will be done. In most cases, symptoms like pale complexion and fatigue appear only when the condition is severe. It is important to identify iron-deficiency anemia early. If the condition is left untreated, your child's growth can be impaired, his intellect impeded, and his resistance to infection diminished. A short attention span and hyperactive behavior can sometimes be a symptom, even in mild cases.

Poor diet is the factor most often linked with this anemia, but it is not the exclusive cause. Children born prematurely or at a low birth weight are automatically at increased risk; some babies even of normal birth weight and gestational age are born with inadequate iron stores because maternal supplies during pregnancy were not adequate. The presence of infection or illness can cause an iron deficiency, too.

Once the condition is identified, the pediatrician is likely to recommend an iron supplement, usually in the form of iron sulfate. Your child's doctor will repeat the blood test to make sure the condition is improving. In some cases, the iron supplements can cause constipation and even diarrhea and nausea. Switching to a smaller dose or dividing the dose into three smaller ones may alleviate the problem. For best absorption, do not give iron supplements with meals. Do not give an iron supplement unless advised to do so by your pediatrician. In a small segment of the population, supplemental iron can cause an iron overload.

IRON-DEFICIENCY ANEMIA AND THE FOOD CONNECTION

Mothers who stop breast-feeding before their baby is 6 months of age or who exclusively breast-feed their baby past her first birthday increase the risk of iron-deficiency anemia. Breast milk is a superb source of iron and it is better absorbed than the iron in infant formula, but it will not be enough to meet a child's growing need for iron. A good source of iron must be added to a child's diet starting at 6 months of age.

The early introduction of cow's milk—before a child's first birthday—can lead to anemia, too. Cow's milk is a very poor source of iron; it is difficult to digest, causing infants to lose tiny traces of blood, which can contribute to iron-deficiency anemia.

The best sources of iron are those that come from meat and poultry. The form of iron found in animal foods is highly absorbable. Iron from vegetables and grains is not as well absorbed, but even consuming a small amount of meat with grains, beans, or vegetables significantly boosts the iron that is absorbed. There is an unidentified component in meat that enhances iron absorption.

Keep milk in its place. Milk is a good source of protein and calcium, but a poor source of iron, and it can even interfere with iron absorption. Some children are so fond of milk that it replaces foods offering more nutrition. Vitamin C enhances iron absorption; for this reason, real fruit juice, rich in vitamin C, is a good choice at mealtimes. Other foods that inhibit iron include bran and tea.

To prevent iron-deficiency anemia:

▪ When formula is used, make sure it is iron fortified.

- When your baby is 4 to 6 months old, start serving a good iron source to your child daily (see page 6).
- Do not add cow's milk to your child's diet until her first birthday, as it can actually cause iron-deficiency anemia if she drinks it before her digestive system is mature enough to handle it.
- Breast-feed your child as long as possible, adding solid foods to his diet around age 6 months.
- Serve a vitamin C–rich food with every meal.
- Keep your child's milk intake in the range of the amounts suggested on pages 6–7.

IRON CONTENT OF FOODS (1-OUNCE PORTIONS) IN GRAMS

The Recommended Daily Allowance for children aged 1 to 10 is 10 milligrams of iron.

Chicken liver	2.8
Beef liver	2.2
Turkey	1.7
Liverwurst	1.5
Hamburger	1.1
Tuna, canned	.5
Hot dogs	.3
Fish sticks	.1
4 tbsp. dry infant cereal	6.8
½ cup cooked cereal	.7
½ cup Total or Product 19	9.0
½ cup Kellogg's Corn Flakes	.3
½ cup cooked beans	1.3–3.0
¼ cup dried fruit	1.0–1.5

To treat iron-deficiency anemia:

■ Offer a small serving of meat, chicken, or egg at every meal. A slice of deli meat can be served along with a meatless meal like macaroni and cheese.
■ Keep a batch of meatballs in the freezer. Reheat and serve one meatball along with your child's regular lunch or supper.
■ Avoid excessive amounts of tea, including sweetened tea drinks that resemble soda.
■ Temporarily eliminate the use of bran or bran cereals.
■ Offer at least two servings from iron-rich foods (see page 177) every day.
■ If constipation becomes a side effect of the iron supplements, serve prunes, whole grains, and lots of fluids.

HOME COMFORT AND MANAGEMENT TIPS

Iron-deficiency anemia rarely causes discomfort except when blood tests need to be done. Help your child with these by practicing the blowing technique for pain management on page 34. The whole family can support the need for iron by looking at the family diet. Young children are easily influenced by the eating habits of both older siblings and their parents. Many snack foods and beverages are very poor iron sources.

BEEF STEW WITH BUTTERMILK DUMPLINGS

YIELD: 4–6 SERVINGS

This is the very best and easiest stew you will ever assemble. The beef is a superb source of iron and the tomatoes carry vitamin C. The soft, doughy dumplings will be a hit with the family, too.

For the stew:
1 lb. stew beef, cut into bite-sized cubes
¼ cup all-purpose flour, seasoned with salt and pepper
1 tbsp. canola oil
1 28-oz. can crushed tomatoes
2 cups beef broth
2 carrots, peeled and cut into coins
3 potatoes, peeled and cut into cubes
½ cup peas

For the dumplings:
1 cup all-purpose flour
1 tsp. baking powder
1 large egg
½ cup buttermilk or plain yogurt

To make the stew:
1. In a large plastic bag toss the seasoned flour with the meat cubes until they are evenly coated.
2. Heat the oil in a large stew pot. Shake excess flour off the meat, and then brown the meat in the oil.
3. When the meat is browned on all sides, add the tomatoes and beef broth. Bring to a boil, then reduce heat and cook on low for 10 minutes.

4. Add carrots and potatoes, then cook 10 to 15 minutes more or until all vegetables are tender when pierced with a fork.

To make the dumplings:

5. In a bowl, combine the flour and baking powder and mix well.
6. In a separate bowl, mix together the egg and buttermilk.
7. Then pour the egg mixture into the flour mixture and stir until ingredients are well combined.

To complete the dish:

8. stir the peas into the stew.
9. Drop the dumpling batter by spoonfuls onto the hot stew.
10. Cover the pot and cook the stew for 10 minutes. Dumplings should look dry and puffy when done. Serve at once.

MINI MEATBALLS

≻

YIELD: 16 MEATBALLS

This recipe is a great source of iron, and the carrots add a lot of vitamin A. Most children like meatballs and sauce, but if your little one does not like tomato sauce, try the sauce-free variation below.

> 1 lb. ground beef, lean
> 1 cup seasoned bread crumbs
> 2 eggs
> 1/4 cup minced onion
> 1 medium carrot, finely grated
> 1/4 tsp. salt
> 2 cups tomato sauce
> 1 tbsp. olive oil

1. In a large bowl, combine all ingredients and mix until well blended.
2. Shape into 16 meatballs. Brown the meatballs in the oil and add to the prepared tomato sauce.
3. Simmer for 30 minutes. Serve hot on pasta or on slices of Italian bread.

VARIATION: MILD MINI MEATBALLS

1. Prepare the meatballs up to step 2 above, but do not brown.
2. Heat 2 cups of chicken or beef broth to a simmer.
3. Add the prepared meatballs and cook for 8 minutes or until the meatballs are no longer pink inside.

⟊ LACTOSE INTOLERANCE

Lactose intolerance is the most common form of food intolerance. The condition often runs in families and is caused by the absence of the enzyme lactase. It is common in African American children at the age of 3; it becomes common in other children after age 5. Lactase digests the milk sugar lactose. When lactase is not present or is available in only small amounts, lactose is not digested. The undigested lactose passes into the intestine, where it causes such symptoms as recurrent abdominal pain, flatulence, a bloated feeling, cramps, and diarrhea. The more lactose consumed, the worse the symptoms.

A child suffering from these symptoms because of lactose intolerance often has very normal physical examination results. Stool tests and a lactose breath test can confirm the family's suspicions, but the elimination of milk produces such dramatic relief that no tests are needed. A primary lactase deficiency lasts for life, whereas a lactose intolerance caused by extended bouts of diarrhea is often temporary. Once the underlying diarrhea is corrected, a normal diet can be resumed. Treatment of lactose intolerance is based on establishing a lactose tolerance level. It is important for parents and children to understand that *lactose intolerance* is not synonymous with *milk sensitivity*. Milk sensitivity is a reaction, with symptoms that are often more severe than those of lactose intolerance, that results when milk protein is ingested. Lactose intolerance occurs because of an intolerance to the milk sugar, not the protein.

LACTOSE INTOLERANCE AND THE FOOD CONNECTION

Whether lactose intolerance is temporary or a permanent problem, the treatment is the same—restrict lactose-containing foods. Once the diagnosis is made, start the diet immediately. Because lactose intolerance results in diarrhea, nutrient absorption can be effected.

In the beginning, be strict with the diet, but over time, once symptoms have stopped, experiment to establish your child's tolerance level. Many foods that contain lactose can be tolerated when eaten in small amounts or as part of a meal. The lactose in yogurt and cheese is fermented and often well tolerated. Lactase enzymes available in tablet form at most pharmacies can be taken before eating a dairy product to assist with digestion of lactose. Cooked milk—as in hot chocolate, pudding, and soup—can eventually be tried, too. Goat's and sheep's milk contain lactose, so they should be consumed as cautiously as cow's milk.

Because a lactose-free diet eliminates dairy products, a superb source of calcium, the risk of a low calcium intake is significant. Calcium is essential for proper bone growth and it helps with muscle contractions and seems to play a role in controlling blood pressure and preventing cancer. The commercially treated lactose-free milks are as good a source of calcium as is untreated cow's milk. In some cases, a calcium supplement may be required; if so, follow the instructions on the label. Children over age 6 can try Rolaids or Tums as an alternative calcium source; again, follow dose recommendations on the label.

THE LACTOSE-FREE DIET

If you must give your child a lactose-free diet, here are some guidelines:

▪ **Milk, yogurt, and cheese group**
  Allowed: lactose-free commercial milk, soy milk
  Avoid: all types of milk and milk products, including canned milk, cocoa mixes, cheese, creamed soup, puddings, and yogurt

▪ **Meat, poultry, fish, dry beans, eggs, and nuts group**
  Allowed: beef, fish, chicken, ham, lamb, eggs (plain or

prepared with allowed ingredients), some cold cuts, peanut butter (natural), tofu

Avoid: creamed and breaded meat, fish, or poultry; baby-food meat with milk added; cheese; eggs (made with cheese or milk); cold cuts made with milk solids

■ **Vegetable Group**
Allowed: all plain vegetables and potatoes
Avoid: creamed vegetables and potatoes and those products processed with milk or prepared with butter or cheese

■ **Fruit group**
Allowed: all fruits, fresh, frozen, or canned
Avoid: frozen and canned fruits processed with lactose

■ **Bread, cereal, rice, and pasta group**
Allowed: bread and rolls made without milk, bagels, pita bread, French bread, Italian bread, hard rolls, pasta, rice, spaghetti
Avoid: bread and rolls made with milk; dried cereals or instant cereals made with milk; crackers, pasta, and rice prepared with milk or cheese; baking mixes and frozen products made with milk

■ **Fats, oils, and sweets group**
Allowed: margarine without butter or milk added; non-dairy creamers, shortening, vegetable oils, some salad dressings; angel food cake, cake, and cookies made without milk; Italian ice; frozen fruit bars; pudding made with water or nondairy creamer; nondairy whipped topping
Avoid: cream, sweet or sour; butter or margarine made with some butter; salad dressings containing milk, cheese, or cream; ice cream or sherbet; butterscotch, caramels, and artificial sweeteners containing lactose; chocolate candy

HOME COMFORT AND MANAGEMENT TIPS

The identification of lactose as the cause of digestive problems is often a relief to parents. A lactose-free diet can be difficult for school-age children to follow because of all the away-from-home meals and snacks. Educate your child about the diet and develop lactose-free alternatives.

Managing lactose intolerance includes the following measures:

■ Frequent diaper changes and tepid baths can relieve diaper rash caused by frequently acid stools.
■ Read food labels and teach your child to read them. Look for milk ingredients.
■ Keep a food journal to identify problematic foods and tolerated foods.
■ Tell day-care providers and schools about your child's need to avoid milk.

LACTOSE CONTENT OF MILK AND MILK PRODUCTS

These foods contain the same amount of lactose as a ½-cup serving of whole milk, skim milk, or buttermilk.

2 tbsp. evaporated milk	1 cup ice cream
3 oz. processed cheese or cheese spread	1 cup ice milk
½ cup half and half	¾ cup sour cream
½ cup plain yogurt	¾ cup whipping cream (light or heavy)

CALCIUM CONTENT OF FOODS

250 mg per serving
1 cup almonds
1 cup cooked collards
1 cup cooked dandelion
  greens
4 oz. self-rising flour
3 oz. sardines

150 mg per serving
1 cup oysters
1 cup cooked rhubarb
3 oz. canned salmon with
  bones
1 cup cooked spinach

100 mg per serving
10 Brazil nuts
1 medium stalk broccoli
1 cup instant farina
3 oz. canned herring
1 tbsp. blackstrap
  molasses
3 tbsp. regular molasses
1 cup cooked navy beans
3.5 oz. tofu
3.5 oz. sunflower seeds
5 tbsp. maple syrup

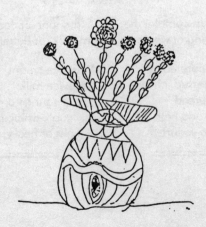

RECIPES

BROWN-SUGAR CUPCAKES

YIELD: 12 CUPCAKES

This basic cupcake requires no frosting—the brown-sugar topping takes care of that.

1 cup granulated sugar
¹/₂ cup margarine
1 ¹/₂ cups all-purpose flour
1 ¹/₂ tsp. baking powder
2 large eggs
¹/₂ cup soy milk
¹/₄ cup brown sugar (for topping)

1. Preheat oven to 350°.
2. Cream the sugar and margarine together until it is light and smooth.
3. Combine the flour with the baking powder.
4. In a small bowl, mix the soy milk and eggs until they are well combined.
5. Alternate adding the soy milk and flour mixture to the creamed sugar until all ingredients are combined and the batter is smooth.
6. Pour batter into greased cupcake tins. Sprinkle each cupcake with an equal amount of brown sugar.
7. Bake for 18 minutes.

SO-GOOD SOY PANCAKES

YIELD: 12 PANCAKES

Soy milk can be used cup for cup to replace cow's milk in almost any recipe. Here, it makes a pancake that your kids will request again and again.

> *2 cups all-purpose flour*
> *5 tsp. granulated sugar*
> *½ tsp. salt*
> *2 tsp. baking powder*
> *1 stick margarine, melted*
> *2 eggs, separated*
> *2 cups soy milk*

1. Sift the flour, sugar, salt, and baking powder together.
2. Combine the melted margarine, egg yolks, and milk together and beat until the yolk is well blended.
3. Stir the soy-milk mixture into the flour until ingredients are well combined, but do not overmix.
4. Beat the egg whites until they form stiff peaks.
5. Gently fold egg whites into the batter—do not overmix.
6. Pour batter into pancakes on a hot, greased griddle; cook until golden. Serve with your best maple syrup.

NOT-REALLY-CHEESECAKE TARTS

These are more than just a cheesecake-like substitute. They are creamy and mildly sweet, with a very light texture not found in ordinary cheesecake. These make a good dessert to bring to parties or school functions.

>*15 gingersnaps*
>*15 miniature muffin cups*
>*1 lb. firm tofu*
>*1 tbsp. lemon juice*
>*¼ cup granulated sugar*
>*1 tsp. vanilla*
>*1 egg*
>*1 cup prepared cherry pie filling (optional)*

1. Preheat the oven to 350°F. Place a gingersnap in the bottom of each muffin cup and arrange cups on a cookie sheet.
2. In a food processor fitted with a steel blade, combine all remaining ingredients and purée until very smooth.
3. With a small ladle or spoon, pour a spoonful of the batter into each gingersnap-lined muffin cup. Each one should be ¾ full.
4. Bake for 20 minutes. After the first 10 minutes of cooking top each tart with 1 tbsp. prepared pie filling; bake tarts another 10 minutes, until they are firm and their tops are bubbly. Cool before serving.

⟡ LEAD POISONING

There are 3.8 million U.S. homes with decaying or deteriorating lead paint, and 2 million children under age 6 live in them. Young children are at a greater risk of lead poisoning than adults because they are likely to chew or put lead-contaminated items in their mouths. Lead in dust and soil can cling to toys, hands, and clothing. Children are affected by lead because they absorb more lead into their small bodies than adults and their brains are still growing. Lead poisoning can interfere with growth and development.

The symptoms of lead poisoning can include fatigue, paleness, constipation, loss of appetite, anemia, memory loss, and sleep disorders. Many states—but not all—require routine lead screening to be included as part of infants' physical examinations. If blood test results show a level of lead above 10 micrograms per deciliter, you need to find the lead source. Your physician will help you contact the local health department for aid in doing so. It takes 1 to 3 weeks of exposure to lead in the environment to raise blood lead levels. A test for iron-deficiency anemia will be ordered, too, because lead interferes with the iron-carrying component in blood called hemoglobin, meaning that iron deficiency often coincides with lead poisoning.

If the blood lead levels are found to be elevated, it can mean anything from mild to severe poisoning. In mild cases, the pediatrician is likely to provide the family with information on ways to reduce lead in the environment and encourage a diet that reduces lead absorption. Later, a repeat test will be done to make sure these measures are working. In severe cases, more aggressive treatment is needed. A drug known as EDTA (ethylenediaminetetraacetic acid) is given by injection, or an intravenous form may be used. EDTA binds with lead and pulls it out of the soft tissues; this is known as chelation therapy. Prompt and aggressive treatment of severe lead poisoning is essential in young children, because in severe cases, it can cause damage such as seizures and mental retardation. Underlying illness, such as sickle cell anemia, can make lead poisoning more severe. Results of tests of lead levels in hair and fingernails do not correlate well with results of blood tests except in severe cases. For this reason, these tests are not useful in identifying or treating lead poisoning, and treatment decisions should not be based upon hair and fingernail tests alone.

To help doctors and families identify children at risk for lead poisoning, researchers at the University of Rochester School of Medicine and Dentistry in Rochester, New York, came up with some key questions to identify kids at risk. If you answer yes to any of the following questions, discuss the need for a lead screening with your pediatrician.

- Does your child live in or regularly visit a house built before 1960 that has peeling or chipping paint?
- Does your child live in or regularly visit a house built before 1960 with recent, ongoing, or planned renovations or remodeling?
- Does your child have a brother, sister, or housemate or playmate with lead poisoning?
- Does your child live with an adult whose job or hobby involves exposure to lead?
- Does your child live near an industry that is likely to release lead (such as a battery plant or a manufacturing plant where lead may be used)?

LEAD POISONING AND THE FOOD CONNECTION

Poor nutrition can enhance lead absorption and toxicity. An important prevention step is to feed your child—at any age—a diet adequate in all nutrients, particularly iron and calcium. It is not uncommon for children with lead poisoning to be deficient in iron, too. In iron-deficient children, 50 percent of the lead they ingest can be absorbed; a diet with adequate iron content reduces that rate to 10 percent.

Calcium offers a similar protective effect. A diet adequate in zinc can be helpful, too, because a zinc deficiency can enhance tissue accumulation of lead and sensitivity to its effects. An effective way to prevent lead poisoning is to feed your child a healthy diet. If your child has lead poisoning, follow your doctor's medical and nutritional advice and include the following dietary strategies:

■ To reduce the amount of lead absorbed from the environment, encourage three small meals plus snacks. More lead is absorbed on an empty stomach than a full one.
■ Foods high in fat help the body absorb dangerous lead faster. Bake, broil, or steam foods instead of frying.
■ Serve two good vitamin C sources every day. This will improve iron absorption.
■ Serve at least two good calcium sources daily, such as milk, yogurt, or cheese.
■ Serve a diet rich in iron, and include one serving of meat, poultry, or fish daily.
■ Serve foods rich in zinc, such as oysters, crab, dark-meat poultry, beef, pork, liver, and bran flakes.

WATER AND LEAD

Infants are at great risk of lead poisoning if their water supply carries lead. In 1989, doctors at Boston Children's Hospital (Boston, Massachusetts) discovered that infants with lead poisoning were drinking formula reconstituted with lead-contaminated water. To reduce the risk of lead poisoning from water, practice the following habits:

■ Do not use the water first drawn in the morning to mix formula or for cooking or drinking.
■ Run tap water for 2 minutes before using it.
■ Decrease your emphasis on using only boiled water for infants. Excessive boiling concentrates lead.

- Discard any lead-based kettles that might be used for boiling.
- Use cold—not hot—tap water for cooking or in food preparation.
- Have your water supply tested for lead—contact your county health department.
- Consider buying bottled water if you think your water pipes carry lead.

HOME MANAGEMENT TIPS

Household paint sold since the mid-1970s does not contain lead. In houses built before 1960, wash hard surfaces, such as floors and window sills, with a high-phosphate solution. Some dishwasher soaps have a high phosphate content; choose one with a "P" code—not "O" code—on the label. Use ¼ cup dishwasher soap in 1 gallon of water. High-phosphate soaps can also be purchased from the hardware store. Other ways to reduce your family's contact with lead include the following:

- Do not sand or remove old paint with a heat gun.
- Get rid of improperly lead-glazed pottery. Pottery made in China and Mexico is likely to contain lead; don't use it in cooking or serving food.
- Wash your hands—and your child's—frequently.
- Wash teething rings and toys frequently.
- If adults in the house work with lead, ask them to shower at work or change before coming into the house.
- Contact your state public health department for more information.

RECIPE

BAKED MANICOTTI WITH MEAT SAUCE

YIELD: 2–3 SERVINGS

Italian food is a classic kid-pleaser. This dish combines cheese (a good source of calcium), ground beef (rich in iron), and a traditional tomato sauce (it's packed with vitamin C). Best of all, your kids will ask for second helpings.

> *8 oz. ground beef*
> *1 27-oz. jar spaghetti sauce*
> *16 oz. part skim ricotta cheese*
> *1 large egg*
> *¹/₂ tsp. garlic powder*
> *1¹/₂ cups grated mozzarella cheese*
> *10 manicotti shells*

1. Cook the manicotti shells per package instructions and set aside.
2. Brown the hamburger meat in its own juices. With a spoon, mash any large lumps.
3. Drain the fat, add the sauce, and cook for 3 minutes. Remove from heat and set aside.
4. Preheat the oven to 350°F.
5. Combine the ricotta cheese, garlic, egg, and 1 cup of mozzarella cheese and blend well.
6. With a spoon or a pastry bag, fill each shell with an equal amount of the prepared cheese mixture.
7. Arrange the shells in a lightly buttered casserole dish. Pour the sauce over the filled shells and sprinkle with remaining mozzarella cheese.
8. Cover dish with aluminum foil and bake for 45 minutes. Let rest for 15 minutes before serving.

SHEPHERD'S PIE

YIELD: 4 INDIVIDUAL PIES

This recipe is a replication of one I remember from my elementary-school cafeteria. It's the kind of recipe kids either love or hate. My kids love it—they particularly enjoy it when they get their own little pot that they don't have to share. The ratio of vegetables to meat is 3 to 1, making this a good way for kids to get their veggies, too.

> 1 lb. lean ground beef
> 2 tbsp. catsup
> 3 or 4 large russet potatoes, peeled
> 1 tbsp. butter
> 1/4–1/2 cup milk
> 1/2 cup corn kernels, fresh or frozen
> 1/2 cup peas, fresh or frozen

1. In a saucepan, brown the ground beef for 5 to 8 minutes until most of the pink color is gone. Drain the fat. Stir in the catsup, remove from heat, and set aside.
2. Place the whole potatoes in a pot filled with enough water to cover them. Bring water to a boil, and cook potatoes for 10 to 15 minutes or until they are tender when pierced with a fork.
3. Mash the potatoes with the butter and enough of the milk to make them smooth.
4. Butter 4 1-cup-capacity custard cups or miniature soufflé dishes. Equally divide the meat mixture between the 4 cups. On top of the meat, place the corn and peas in equal portions on each dish. Top with an equal amount of potatoes.
5. Bake for 25 minutes at 350°F. If your child does not like a crispy crust, cover the pies with aluminum foil while cooking.

⤬⟋ NAUSEA

If you're lucky, you will spot nausea symptoms before they lead to vomiting. If your child looks pale and feels sweaty and maybe dizzy, he is likely to be feeling nauseated. Nausea is common in kids, and may be due to a stomach-ache, motion sickness, or a disgusting sight or smell. Nausea and motion sickness can occur during a boat, car, or train ride. Looking at fast-moving scenery seems to make the condition worse. It probably begins with a disturbance in the fluid balance of the inner ear, which causes the brain to tell the stomach that something is wrong, which results in nausea and vomiting.

In most cases, nausea is self-limiting and motion sickness can often be prevented. If nausea continues for more than 1 or 2 days, consult your health-care provider. Nausea can be the cause of poor nutrition. If it is accompanied by vomiting, dehydration is a risk.

NAUSEA AND THE FOOD CONNECTION

When nausea occurs, hold off on the solids and offer tepid liquids. A defizzed carbonated beverage (leave beverage uncovered to help it go flat) is soothing and helpful in controlling symptoms. Light, low-fat snacks, such as bread sticks, saltines, pretzels, and plain cereal might be well tolerated, but avoid heavy meals. Dietary measures you can take include the following:

■ Offer only clear liquids until the nausea passes.
■ To prevent nausea due to motion sickness, try serving plain saltines while driving or boating.
■ Chewing gum may help your child during car trips.
■ Avoid serving foods with a strong odor.
■ A food or beverage consumed right before your child vomits may carry an unpleasant association with it. Do not offer this food again until your child feels better.

HOME COMFORT AND MANAGEMENT TIPS

If your child is feeling nauseated, let her lie down with her eyes open. Open up a window to get her some fresh air. When she's ready, take a walk with her or put her in a stroller.

To prevent motion sickness:

- Keep your child in a car seat, even when he's old enough to wear a seat belt. The seats reduce the incidence of motion sickness because they force children to sit upright.
- Ask your child not to read while the car is moving.
- If in a plane or boat, sit with your child in the most stable spot. Don't let your child go below deck, as this is the most likely spot to induce seasickness.
- Do not use motion sickness patches on your child—the doses are for adults only.
- Prepare for the worst. Keep a supply of plastic bags and wet wipes on hand.
- If your child is to be traveling with friends or Grandma and Grandpa, make sure they know of her tendency to become car-sick. Ask that they make frequent stops.

ᕦ SLEEP

Sleep is not a problem—the lack of it is. Parents of newborns say their own sleep deprivation and their baby's nighttime waking are sources of huge stress. In the first week of life, infants sleep over 16 hours a day, but with each passing week, their need for sleep ever so slightly declines and they become more interested in their environment—meaning they're often more wakeful at unwanted times. As children get older, stress can cause insomnia. Yes, even children experience stress, caused by things such as toilet training, fear of separation from Mom and Dad, and first-day-of-school jitters. Illness, such as an ear infection,

INSOMNIA (HYPOSOMNIA)

If your child has trouble falling asleep, staying asleep, or wakes very early in the morning, he might have insomnia, the inability to sleep as desired. Not all sleep troubles are due to true insomnia; some are due to normal development. For example, it is common for 9- and 10-month-olds to experience a period of nighttime wakefulness, and up to two-thirds of all 5-year-olds can take 30 minutes to fall asleep at night.

If a medical problem is a cause of your child's insomnia (ear, nose, and throat symptoms often are), your child will usually have symptoms during the day as well as night. Sleep apnea, a potentially serious breathing problem that disturbs sleep, is symptomatic only at night. The problem can often be identified by parents who hear marked snoring or gasping sounds that precede night wakings. This condition must be treated with the help of a doctor.

Anxiety almost always leads to sleep disturbances. Even children in the most stable and supportive families really do worry a lot. Kids with insomnia can actually become preoccupied with falling asleep, which only makes matters worse.

If your child has insomnia, first consider possible medical causes, including any medications she is taking. Look to diet: is your child eating too close to bedtime or getting too much caffeine? Is he taking a nap too late in the day? In the vast majority of cases, the cause will not be identified. Offer reassurance. Establish a bedtime routine and follow it. Let your child read in bed or play with a puzzle when he can't get to sleep. Try not to start a hard-to-break habit like getting back out of bed once in it or falling asleep in front of the TV. If your child is an early riser, put books to look at or paper to draw on by the side of his bed. Tell her to use these until she hears the alarm sound in Mommy and Daddy's room. If the problem persists, discuss it with your child's doctor.

can prevent sleep. At age 3 or 4, night terrors and nightmares can surface.

In most cases, medical complications are rarely the cause of sleep disturbances. Young children need to learn how to fall asleep on their own and that the whole family needs sleep. They must also learn that they are expected to stay in bed once they get there. Parents can do a lot to help children develop good sleeping habits.

SLEEP AND THE FOOD CONNECTION

Many—but not all—babies can sleep through the night by 8 weeks of age. But keep in mind that a night's sleep is defined as midnight to 5 A.M. By age 3 months, 70 percent of babies are sleeping through the night, and by 6 months, that percentage climbs to 83 percent. However, in the second 6 months of life, little ones often become wakeful at night again.

Studies show that formula-fed babies often sleep through the night sooner than their breast-fed contemporaries. Babies need to be fed frequently to establish lactation, but as they get older, night wakefulness may not be due to hunger. To help breast-feeding mothers, researchers at the University of Illinois at Urbana–Champaign conducted a study published in 1993, to evaluate the effectiveness of behavioral techniques in getting babies to sleep longer. The researchers instructed mothers to give their babies a "focal feed" between 10 P.M. and midnight and gradually lengthen intervals between middle-of-the-night feedings by carrying out alternative caretaking activities such as reswaddling, holding, diapering, and walking the baby instead of offering feeding as the first response. If these caretaking activities didn't lead to sleep, then the baby would be fed. An attentive response on the part of mothers can teach an infant that their distress will be attended to but that feeding is not the exclusive response.

Mothers need to follow their own instincts about how to

help their child get a good night's sleep. When you believe it is time to reduce nighttime feedings, the following strategies may be helpful:

■ Increase daytime feeding intervals.
■ Offer the nighttime feeding as late as possible and gradually reduce the amount of formula given or time spent breastfeeding.
■ When your baby cries, check her but do not pick her up or feed her right away. See if reswaddling or even a gentle massage will get her back to sleep. When she is older and on solids and regular meals, food can still effect your child's sleep patterns. Eating too much or consuming caffeine right before bed can prevent sleep. Fluids right before bed can increase the need for nighttime bathroom trips.
■ If you are bottle-feeding, eliminate the nighttime bottle as soon as possible. Even those filled with water can lead to wet diapers that require changing in the middle of the night.
■ If your 6- to 12-month-old suddenly starts to cry at night, he might be experiencing nightmares. This is usually a temporary phase, reassure your child immediately but avoid offering a feeding. Comfort him with soothing words.
■ On a scale of 1 to 10, with 10 being stuffed, keep your child's hunger in the 5 to 6 range before bed.
■ Let supper be the last eating opportuntiy of the day. This is particularly important in children under 9, who need more than 10 hours of sleep each night. A 10-year-old can stay up later; a light snack is probably acceptable for a child of this age.
■ At supper, serve foods rich in tryptophan, which is an amino acid that changes to serotonin and can aid in sleep. In the 1980s, tryptophan supplements were found to cause serious side effects, so these supplements are no

TRYPTOPHAN CONTENT OF FOOD (IN MILLIGRAMS)

American cheese, 1 oz.	92
Cheddar cheese, 3.5 oz.	320
Cottage cheese, 4 oz.	150
Egg, 1 large	97
Milk shake, 10 oz.	130
Fish, 3 oz.	160
Apple, 1 medium	3
Spaghetti, 1 cup	58
Hamburger, 3.5 oz.	300
Milk, 8 oz.	115
Yogurt, 8 oz.	67
Eggnog, 8 oz.	137
Cream soup, 1 cup	30
Tofu, ½ cup	156
Turkey, 3.5 oz.	325

longer available, but tryptophan is available naturally in food. In its natural form, there is no risk of side effects.

HOME COMFORT AND MANAGEMENT TIPS

Parents can help children sleep well by setting a reasonable sleep schedule and then sticking with it. You cannot make your child go to sleep, but you can expect her to get in and stay in bed—sleep will follow. A schedule and sleep routine will take the stress and fatigue out of your night—for you and for your child. Keep in mind that children do need their sleep and you are doing your child a great service by helping her get it. If she is well rested, she will do better in school, have better personal relationships, and resist illness more effectively. To help your child sleep better, try the following measures:

- Give your infant a cuddly child-safe object to sleep with.
- Try using white noise for your infants.
- Put your child in bed awake. If he routinely falls asleep elsewhere and not in his bed, he may develop inappropriate sleep associations.
- If your child refuses to go to sleep, compare his nap and sleep schedule to the recommended sleep requirements on page 203.
- Move naps to earlier in the day if they are interfering with bedtime.
- If your child always asks for items that prolong the nighttime routine, try to think ahead: put a glass of water by the bed or her favorite blanket or toy by her side. When your nighttime routine is over—reading, washing, brushing teeth—ask your little one if there is anything else she needs. Tell her this is her last opportunity for requests. Then leave the room. If another request is made, tell her she will have to wait until the morning because now it is time for sleep.
- Nighttime fears are real for children. Reassure your child. Listen to his concerns, look under the bed for any monsters, and keep a night light on.
- Don't let your child watch scary cartoons or even shows with fictitious monsters in them before bed. If your child is in the room, stay away from the cops-and-robbers shows and the evening news, too.
- To reduce the risk of sudden infant death syndrome (SIDS), the AAP now urges parents to place their infants on their side or backs when putting them down to sleep: this way, their noses aren't buried in blankets, which can cut off their air supply.

RECOMMENDED SLEEP REQUIREMENTS

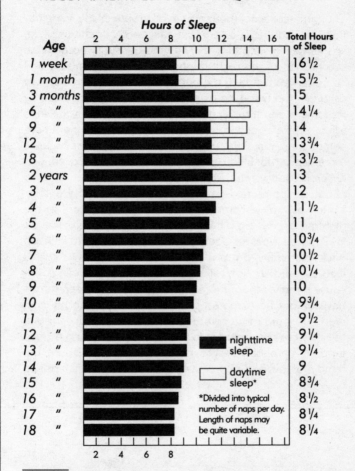

Hours of Sleep

Age	Total Hours of Sleep
1 week	16½
1 month	15½
3 months	15
6 "	14¼
9 "	14
12 "	13¾
18 "	13½
2 years	13
3 "	12
4 "	11½
5 "	11
6 "	10¾
7 "	10½
8 "	10¼
9 "	10
10 "	9¾
11 "	9½
12 "	9¼
13 "	9¼
14 "	9
15 "	8¾
16 "	8½
17 "	8¼
18 "	8¼

■ nighttime sleep

□ daytime sleep*

*Divided into typical number of naps per day. Length of naps may be quite variable.

Reprinted with permission from Ferber, R.: *Solve Your Child's Sleep Problems*. New York: Simon & Schuster, 1985.

NIGHTMARES AND NIGHT TERRORS

Though these scary thoughts are all in your child's imagination, they can have a very real effect on your child's sleep, so they need your attention. Nightmares usually occur in the second half of the night during the deep-sleep phase and can often be recalled in great detail. A sleep terror usually occurs in the first 4 hours of sleep and is accompanied by screaming and thrashing. During a sleep terror, your child will most likely not be aware of your presence. A nightmare can be more disruptive of sleep than a sleep terror because it seems so vivid. Sleep terrors often cannot be recalled, and children usually return to sleep quickly. Reassure children about a nightmare; some kids want to share the details. I often ask my children to describe the ''monster'' in the nightmare. How big is he? What color is he? Where does he live? These types of questions seem to bring my children back into reality, but you'll have to follow your own child's lead. Some kids don't like to talk about scary things because it makes them more real. My children's sleep terrors have always been more upsetting to me than to my children. They are more common in a three- or four-year-old, but they are not exclusive to this age group. During a sleep terror, it is probably best to make sure your child is safe, but remain uninvolved and allow your child to fall back asleep on his own.

RECIPES

TOWER OF TURKEY

YIELD: 1 SANDWICH

A turkey sandwich accompanied by a cold glass of milk has long been a remedy for sleeplessness. Research says it is the natural tryptophan contained in the turkey and milk that aids sleep; I think it might also just be the wholesome goodness in the combination.

> *Cold sliced turkey*
> *2 slices crispy bacon*
> *Lettuce*
> *Sliced tomato*
> *Mayonnaise*
> *1 large soft roll, cut into 3 slices, not 2*

1. On the first layer, spread some mayonnaise. Add tomato slices and the bacon. Top with the middle slice of roll.
2. Spread a smidge more mayonnaise on the middle layer and add the turkey slices. Cover with the remaining top of the roll and enjoy! With a glass of milk, of course.

GOOD-NIGHT MILK

Plain milk, cold or warm, is certainly a great drink, and it truly can help kids get to sleep. Try one of these variations for when you want something different.

MALTED MILK

YIELD: 1 SERVING

Served hot or ice cold, malted milk is great. Malt powder is available at the many supermarkets or specialty stores.

> $2/3$ *cups milk*
> *2–3 tbsp. malt powder*

1. Combine ingredients in a tall glass.
2. Serve cold.

STEAMED MILK

YIELD: 1 SERVING

To prepare a true steamed milk, you will need an espresso maker, but if that is not available, a suitable alternative can be created by scalding the milk and removing any skin that forms. Vanilla syrup is available at specialty coffeehouses.

> $2/3$ *cups milk*
> *1–2 tbsp. vanilla syrup*

1. Prepare the milk in the espresso machine or bring the milk to a boil in a small saucepan.
2. Pour the hot milk into a mug and add the syrup. Serve warm.

⤬ SORE THROAT

Sore throats often accompany colds and they are particularly common in children ages 5 and 10. Symptoms include pain, difficulty swallowing, swelling, and redness. If a sore throat comes on gradually, the cause is likely to be a virus; sudden symptoms accompanied by fever, swollen glands, and headache are often suspected to be caused by bacteria. Strep throat is caused by bacteria and requires antibiotic therapy. If your child has been exposed to strep throat, has a rash, spots in the mouth, or any underlying condition, alert your doctor so the proper treatment can be started. Mononucleosis, another familiar childhood ailment, can also cause sore throat symptoms. Dust, smoke, and chemicals can cause a sore throat; even sleeping with an open mouth because of having a stuffed-up nose can cause the problem.

SORE THROAT AND THE FOOD CONNECTION

Moisture and soothing foods will help ease your child's sore throat. Warm fluids will keep mucous membranes moist, and warm gargles give temporary relief to dry, irritated throats. Soft, nonirritating foods, such as soup, ice cream, and custard, may be preferred by your child. Dietary measures you can take include the following:

■ Offer plenty of fluids—enough so that your child's urine is clear and light-colored.
■ If your child does not like salt, try a gargle of warm water mixed with 1 or 2 teaspoons of corn syrup or molasses. Young kids like this better and it is just as effective.
■ Offer tea with honey, warm cider, or a mock toddy (recipes are all included in Chapter 4).
■ Ice-cold foods, such as ice cream or fruit ice pops, can help numb an aching throat, and they provide fluid, too.

- Citrus fluids, such as orange or grapefruit juice, should be temporarily halted because they can hurt an already sore throat. Vitamin C is still essential, so serve a vitamin C–fortified apple juice or cranberry juice.

HOME COMFORT AND MANAGEMENT TIPS

If your child gets lots of sore throats, humidity—or the lack of it—might be a contributor. Comfort measures you can try include the following:

- Keep your child away from irritating fumes or substances.
- Use a cool-mist humidifier. A cold-water humidifier is preferred over a hot-water vaporizer in case it tips over.
- Avoid dusty places, such as gymnastic rooms that can carry chalk dust—used to enhance gripping—in the air.
- Try slivers of hard candy or throat lozenges for moisture. Avoid the hard, round type because of the risk of choking.

RECIPES

PEPPERMINT FRAPPÉ

YIELD: 1 SERVING

Peppermint has a "cool" taste in the mouth and is a natural for relieving a sore throat.

2/3 cup milk
2 tbsp. peppermint flavoring
1/4 cup vanilla or mint ice cream

1. Combine all ingredients in a blender and purée until smooth.
2. Serve right away.

PEPPERMINT FRUIT TWISTS

YIELD: 1 SERVING

The sauce starts off creamy when hot, but forms a thin, re-freshing coating over the fruit as it cools. The sauce tastes great served on ice cream, too.

3 peppermint patties
1 tbsp. cream or milk
5 or 6 large strawberries, washed, with the green top still on

1. In a small saucepan, combine the patties and the cream. On low heat, melt the patties until they are smooth and creamy.
2. Dip the strawberries into the sauce so that two thirds of each berry is covered.
3. Place berries on a glass plate or on wax paper. Refrigerate and serve when the sauce has hardened.

✑ STOMACHACHES (ABDOMINAL PAIN)

School-aged children get lots of stomachaches, but in only about 5 percent of cases can a cause be identified. A stomachache can actually be located anywhere along the lower digestive tract, including the stomach and intestines. A food intolerance can cause cramping that occurs in the intestines but is described as appearing in the stomach. Stomachache can be an early sign of flu or even food poisoning. In most cases, indigestion, overeating, constipation, or stress is the likely cause, but abdominal pain can also indicate serious underlying problems, including disease or infection. Do not ignore recurrent or persistent abdominal pain. Food poisoning often carries stomachache symptoms, too.

Contact a physician if a stomachache persists or is accompanied by fever, vomiting, or diarrhea. The doctor may order blood and urine tests to aid in diagnosis. When there is no organic cause behind a persistent stomachache, emotional factors may be involved. Suspect an emotional cause if the stomachache occurs along with other problems, such as school or sleep problems, or difficulties with family or peers. If the root of the problem is emotional, this does not mean the pain is imaginary. An emotionally induced stomachache requires treatment, too. Young children, particularly school-aged, children, are under a lot of stress. Discuss this with your child.

The use of acetaminophen is not recommended for the treatment of stomachaches. If no underlying cause is established, look to your child's diet to make things better.

STOMACHACHES AND THE FOOD CONNECTION

If there is no medical reason that can explain your child's stomachache, examine what she is eating. Lack of fiber, lack of fluids, irregular meals, or even over- or undercon-sumption can be a cause of a stomachache. The feeding suggestions below should be tried when your physician has ruled out any medical reason for the stomachache. The idea is to get your child on a diet that aids digestion and regular bowel movements.

- If your child's stomach is really sore, offer clear liquids until she feels better.
- Start a regular meal schedule. Encourage your child to eat even-sized meals, not over- or undereating at any given meal.
- Be sure your child is eating the recommended servings of fruit from Chapter 1 that match his age (see pages 6–7).
- Try adding a banana a day to your child's menu. Not only does it contain fiber, but results of at least one study have shown a banana can help indigestion.
- If your child is a fast eater, ask her to slow down.
- Allow enough time for eating and create a relaxed envi-ronment.
- If your child is a frequent gum chewer or candy sucker, he may be swallowing air, which creates gas in the stom-ach and stomach pain—have him discontinue the prac-tice and see if it helps.
- Is your child eating a lot of gas-producing vegetables, such as broccoli, cauliflower, Brussels sprouts, or baked beans, or has the family suddenly started a high-fiber diet? Do not eliminate these foods, but use them more judiciously until your child becomes accustomed to them.
- Write down the foods your child has eaten in the hours preceding the stomachache. Be particular about fluids consumed. Some fruit juices, artificially flavored drinks, or artificially sweetened desserts can cause a stomach-ache.
- Is your child consuming a lot of concentrated sweets? Milk shakes and soda, consumed in large amounts (over

8 ounces), can rapidly put a large dose of sweet carbohydrates in your child's stomach, leading to a stomachache.
■ Chili powder, black pepper, caffeine, and chocolate can irritate the stomach lining, and these should be temporarily eliminated. Excessive caffeine has no place in a child's diet.

HOME COMFORT AND MANAGEMENT TIPS

Do not use any nonprescription stomach remedies unless so advised by your doctor. Let proper diet, rest, and time help a tummy-ache—it almost always does. Some additional nondrug remedies you can use include the following:

■ A hot-water bottle placed on the tummy is very soothing to children.
■ Make time for regular bowel movements.
■ When you suspect stress is the cause, gentle exercise, such as a walk with Mom and Dad, may help relieve some of the tension. Dancing can be a good muscle relaxer, too. The sound track from a children's movie can get your child moving, and the movement can relax muscles.
■ Cuddles can help relieve stress.

RECIPES

BROILED BANANAS

YIELD: 1 SERVING

This recipe is simple but good. Bananas are very digestible and soothing. Certainly, bananas are good all by themselves, but occasionally warm, dressed-up fruit is more appealing and comforting than cold fruit.

> *1 medium banana, firm—even a bit on the green side*
> *1 tbsp. brown sugar*
> *¼ cup plain or vanilla yogurt*

1. Peel and cut the banana in half. Sprinkle both sides with the brown sugar.
2. Place banana under a broiler for 3 minutes or until the brown sugar melts and bubbles.
3. Remove from the broiler and serve warm, with the yogurt.

VERY VEGETABLE SOUP

YIELD: 3 CUPS

Soup can be a great vehicle for serving vegetables. Children often like raw vegetables, but when they are ill, they seem more likely to eat cooked vegetables.

> *1 small onion, chopped*
> *3 cups hot chicken stock*
> *1 carrot, peeled and diced*
> *1 stalk celery, chopped*
> *¹/₂ cup potatoes, peeled and diced*

1. Sauté the onion in 2 tbsp. of the chicken stock, until the onion is soft and translucent.
2. Pour in all the stock and the remaining vegetables.
3. Simmer, covered, for 25 minutes. Serve warm.

POACHED PEARS

YIELD: 2 SERVINGS

This is a wonderful fruit dessert. The brown sugar syrup makes the pears deliciously sweet and it is very easy to prepare.

> **2 whole pears, peeled and cored and sliced in half**
> **¹/₄ cup brown sugar**
> **1 clove**
> **1 cup water**

1. In a saucepan, combine the sugar, cloves, and water. Cook until the sugar melts.
2. Put the pears in a microwave-safe dish, pour the sugar water over them, and cover. Cook in the microwave, on high, for 3 minutes. Remove the pears from the oven and let them rest for 3 minutes to complete cooking.
3. Serve warm with a generous topping of the poaching syrup.

❧ TEETHING

Teething is the natural eruption of teeth—when you think about the process, it is surprising that it isn't the cause of even more discomfort than it is. By the time your child is 3 years old, 20 primary teeth will have emerged, usually beginning around 4 months of age, but starting in some babies in the first month. Teething can make for a cranky, uncomfortable infant, but it is usually not responsible for significant fever. Sometimes a runny nose, diarrhea, or even a rash can accompany the process.

There is no treatment for teething. The doctor may recommend acetaminophen for pain relief, but in many cases, teething pain cannot be distinguished from other causes of infant fussiness, so treatment with pain relief may be fruitless. Orajel or Anbesol are baby teething jels that can provide limited and temporary relief. Follow the package instructions for proper use.

Teething babies love to put things in their mouth to ease the soreness of their gums. Unfortunately, this means they come in contact with illness-causing germs or even lead from lead-contaminated dust or soil.

TEETHING AND THE FOOD CONNECTION

Cold, chewy food can give relief to sore gums. Since teething first begins when infants are still on formula or breast milk, be careful not to use any foods that might be too difficult for an infant to manipulate. Even a bread stick can turn into a gooey clump that can be difficult to swallow. Don't leave your little one unattended while she is chomping on a teething food. As soon as teeth start to emerge, begin a routine dental program. Though many mothers fear that teething may be a reason to terminate breast feeding it rarely is. You can teach your baby not to bite while he nurses by using your pinkie finger to gently break the seal of his mouth on your breast whenever he tries out his teeth on you. He'll learn relatively quickly.

Try these teething foods:

- Frozen bagels
- Frozen banana
- Homemade Teething Biscuits (see recipe on page 218)
- Pretzel Rings (see recipe on page 219)

HOME COMFORT AND MANAGEMENT TIPS

Other ways to help your teether include the following:

- Cool, firm compresses can help sore gums.
- Rub your child's gums gently with a clean finger.
- Freeze a damp, clean washcloth for baby to chew on.
- Put crushed ice in a clean sock, tie off the ends, and give it to baby to chomp on.
- Let your baby gnaw on a cold—not frozen—teething ring.
- Drooling, which accompanies teething, can cause a rash. Pat your child's chin dry frequently and put a layer of Vaseline on her chin for protection.
- Put Orajel on a toothbrush and let baby chew.
- If your toddler complains about a toothache, look in his mouth to see if there is anything stuck between his teeth. Rinse his mouth out with warm, lightly salted water. Try to swish out any particles. Call the dentist if pain persists.

RECIPES

TEETHING BISCUITS

YIELD: 12 BISCUITS

Store-bought teething biscuits are more convenient, but making your own can be fun. No matter what type you use, they all become very messy after baby has chewed on them for a while.

3 eggs
1 1/2 cups sugar
3 1/2 cups flour

1. Preheat the oven to 275°F.
2. Beat the eggs, add the sugar, and beat the mixture until smooth. Add enough of the flour to make a stiff but not too dry dough.
3. Roll the dough out onto a floured cutting board about 1 in. thick. Cut into 3" × 1" rectangles.
4. Bake the biscuits on a lightly oiled cookie sheet for 3 hours. They will be very firm and hard. Store in an airtight container.

PRETZEL RINGS

YIELD: 8 RINGS

Look like bagels, taste like pretzels.

> *1 cup warm water (95°F to 115°F)*
> *1 package dry yeast*
> *1 tbsp. granulated sugar*
> *1 tbsp. canola oil*
> *2–3 cups all-purpose flour*

1. Combine the sugar and the warm water in a bowl, then sprinkle the yeast on top. Cover the mixture with a paper towel and let it sit in a warm spot for 2 or 3 minutes. Bubbles should form on the surface, and the whole mixture should take on a foamy, spongy look. This means the yeast is growing.
2. In a larger bowl, combine the yeast mixture, oil, and 2 cups of the flour. Stir with a spoon and mixing in enough additional flour so that the dough becomes firm and can hold its shape. Do not add so much flour that it becomes dry and crumbly.
3. On a flour-covered board, knead the dough for a few minutes until it is smooth. Divide the dough into 8 small portions. Roll each portion of dough between your palms until the piece is about 8 in. long. Connect the ends to form a circle. Place the rings on a lightly oiled baking sheet and let them rise for 30 minutes. They will double in size.
4. Bake in a preheated 350°F oven for 20 minutes.

URINARY TRACT INFECTIONS

Cystitis, or inflammation of the bladder, is the most common type of urinary tract infection (UTI). These infections are more common in girls than boys because girls have a shorter urethra, meaning bacteria have a much shorter trip to reach the bladder. A UTI occurs when bacteria multiply to excessive numbers and cause symptoms that can include a need to urinate frequently, painful urination, and fever. UTIs are not always easy for parents to identify. One to 2 percent of infants will get a UTI, with symptoms that include fever, vomiting, or diarrhea, but no urinary symptoms. Up to two-thirds of preschool and school-aged girls who have a UTI can actually be symptom free. Bedwetting in older children can be a sign that an infection is developing in the urinary tract.

Left untreated, UTI could lead to a kidney infection. For proper diagnosis, a urine culture to measure bacteria must be done. If the urine culture shows an abundance of harmful bacteria, antibiotics will be prescribed. It is essential that all of the prescribed medicine be taken, even when symptoms abate. Completing the antibiotic therapy can prevent recurrence. Frequently, a follow-up urine culture will be requested to make sure there are no troublesome bacteria lingering to recreate an infection. Never try to treat a UTI without the help of your health-care provider.

URINARY TRACT INFECTIONS AND THE FOOD CONNECTION

Fluids directly affect the urinary tract, so the type of and volume of fluids taken in can assist in the treatment of a UTI. An increase in fluids can help wash away some bacteria. Cranberry juice has long been the beverage of choice for treating a UTI. The reasons for its effectiveness are not well established, but three factors contribute to its reputation: (1) it is a fluid, and like all fluids, it can dilute urine and flush bacteria; (2) it may contain chemicals that fight bacteria; and (3) it may change the pH of urine, which assists in killing off bacteria. Most children like cranberry juice and it is a good source of vitamin C. A menu high in fiber, with adequate fluid intake, will prevent constipation, which can contribute to the frequency of UTI in some children. Since UTIs frequently recur, proper diet is an important factor in their prevention:

- Encourage your child to drink enough fluids so that her urine is light in color.
- Serve cranberry juice.
- Serve a good vitamin C source with every meal. The best sources include citrus juices and fruits.

HOME COMFORT AND MANAGEMENT TIPS

Other preventive measures include the following:

- Avoid bubble baths, which may increase the risk of a UTI.
- Instruct your young child to completely empty his bladder every time he urinates and make sure he is urinating as frequently as he needs to.
- Have your child wear cotton underwear.
- Avoid tight-fitting clothing.
- Teach your child—especially if she's a little girl—to properly wipe after a bowel movement. Wiping front to back is less likely to contaminate the urethra.
- Discourage extended lounging in a wet bathing suit.

RECIPES

CRANBERRY SUNRISE

YIELD: 1 SERVING

Cranberry juice can get boring if a child is told to drink a lot of it. This combination can be a fun alternative, and it's pretty, too!

Equal amounts of orange and cranberry juices

1. Combine juices in a tall glass.
2. Serve with ice and garnish with an orange.

CRUSHED CRANBERRY CRUNCH

YIELD: 2 SERVINGS

This recipe may not actally cure or prevent an infection, but it tastes good, and both yogurt and cranberries are said to carry infection-fighting properties. What a tasty way to get your medicine!

> 1 cup canned cranberry sauce
> 1 cup plain or vanilla yogurt
> 2 tbsp. granulated sugar
> 1 large orange

1. Form 2 serving cups out of the orange: cut it in half and scrape out all the fruit. Try not to perforate the skin. Set the orange-peel cups aside.
2. Remove all the seeds from the fruit of the orange and any large pieces of the membrane from the orange sections.
3. In a bowl, combine the cranberry sauce, yogurt, and reserved orange pieces. Add enough of the sugar to make it the desired sweetness. Divide this mixture equally between the orange cups.
4. Wrap filled orange-peel cups in plastic and freeze overnight. Allow to thaw 5 minutes and serve as a dessert or snack.

⤝ VOMITING

Though common and a natural protective defense of the body, this is a symptom that is upsetting both to parents and children. Vomiting occurs when all or part of the stomach contents is expelled. It is the body's attempt to rid itself of harmful substances that can include the toxins created by bacteria or a virus, food poisoning, or an irritant that it cannot tolerate. Gastroenteritis and overfeeding are the most common causes. A common cause of vomiting in infants is gastroesophageal reflux, a condition in which the sphincter or "door" that separates the stomach from the esophagus is not closing tightly, allowing the stomach contents to be regurgitated as vomit. This occurs after feeding and can be a source of poor nutrition. Most infants outgrow the problem by the first year, and it can be treated with the help of proper positioning and thickened food. Formula intolerance or, in rare cases, something more serious, such as an obstruction, can be a cause of vomiting in infants. In older children a severe cough or even some medications can cause vomiting.

In most situations vomiting due to illness will resolve itself in one or two days without any medical intervention. In some cases an antiemetic drug may be prescribed. The risk for dehydration is greatest in infants, and parents should always call the pediatrician if their newborn is vomiting. Parents of older children who observe symptoms that include red or brown vomit and abdominal pain—or if vomiting occurs in conjunction with a head injury—call the doctor. If vomiting occurs more than four times in 2 hours, the doctor should be notified then, too.

VOMITING AND THE FOOD CONNECTION

Fluids are essential, but they must not be forced. Too much fluid too soon can lead to more vomiting and increase the risk of dehydration. Hold off on milk and raw fruit or juice, at least temporarily. Water is the best liquid to start with. Dehydration, loss of appetite, and weight loss are all potential side effects of vomiting in children.

If your baby is vomiting because of formula intolerance, discuss the merits of switching to a soy-based formula with your doctor. If vomiting is due to GER, give your baby small, frequent feedings. After feeding, keep him prone, with the head of the bed slightly elevated. Thicker food may help, too. Combine a small amount of infant rice cereal with formula or expressed breast milk. Serve this in a bottle with a hole large enough to accommodate the cereal.

If your child is vomiting because of illness, rest her tummy for 2 hours, but offer 1 to 3 ounces of fluid every hour. Here are some tips:

- Give ice chips—plain or mixed with 1 tablespoon of flat ginger ale—not citrus juice or Gatorade.
- Progress to clear liquids as tolerated: water, plain gelatin, diluted broth, caffeine-free clear soda.
- Avoid extremes in temperatures; large amounts of ice cream or ice water may not be well tolerated.

When the vomiting has stopped and your child has an appetite, progress to simple foods:

- Bananas, rice, applesauce, and toast are time-honored remedies (see BRAT diet, page 119). Crackers or plain baked potatoes are also very soothing.
- Serve bland foods. Read about a bland diet in Chapter 4 (page 229).
- If vomiting occurs after eating solid food, go back to clear fluids (see page 228).
- Keep food portions very small.
- Discuss the use and need for rehydration formulas such as Pedialyte or Rehydralyte with your physician. If re-

quired, they will be better tolerated given in small amounts—one spoonful at a time—instead of in a bottle or cup. Give enough spoonfuls to meet the recommended amount.

■ For your older child, a hard candy or mint can be very refreshing after vomiting. However, thin, flat Life Savers are a better choice than hard, solid, round candies because children are less likely to choke on them.

■ Weight loss due to a short-term illness and vomiting is only temporary. When your child's appetite comes back, resuming her normal diet will lead to proper weight gain.

■ Return to milk products, starting in ½-cup portions, and then proceed as tolerated.

HOME COMFORT AND MANAGEMENT TIPS

Vomiting can be very scary for children. Some even feel bad about making a mess. Reassure your child—do the obvious:

■ Keep a deep pot for vomiting by your child's bed or chair.
■ Keep a box of tissues on hand.
■ Wipe his face with a warm, damp cloth.
■ Keep him warm and comfortable—no tight, restrictive clothes.
■ Air out the room frequently to keep the room smelling fresh.

4

COMFORT FOODS

We all remember how great it was to have our mommies make us something special when we were sick. This chapter contains recipes that have no proven medical benefits, but what they do to light up the face of an ailing child is worth just as much. The recipes in this section are multipurpose sick-day foods. By that I mean they can be prepared for a variety of ailments. For example, a creamy vanilla pudding can be served when chickenpox takes hold or used to help distract a child from the discomfort of a headache. Meat loaf is a great food to serve when iron is needed for iron-deficiency anemia, but lots of kids also find it appropriately bland and appealing as they rebound from the flu. Of course, macaroni and cheese is an all-time childhood favorite that you'll no doubt serve often.

Besides recipes, you'll find information about what to include in liquid and soft, bland diets, which doctors often recommend to treat a number of childhood ailments.

CLEAR LIQUIDS

A menu of clear liquids is nutritionally inadequate and should be used for only short periods. The foods allowed on a clear liquid diet include:

- Clear broth
- Bouillon
- Cranberry juice
- Apple juice
- Grape juice
- Gelatin (not diet)
- Ice water
- Ice pops
- Clear, weak tea
- Carbonated—but defizzed—soda (not diet)—defizz it by leaving it out uncovered

FULL-LIQUID DIET

Foods on this menu may make the transition from liquids to solids easier. It should be used for only short periods of time because it does not contain enough foods to meet a child's nutritional needs. The foods allowed on a full-liquid diet include:

- Formula, breast milk, or milk
- Clear broth or strained, milk-based soup
- Puréed meat, fish, poultry, or egg blended into broth or soup (for children 8 months and older)
- Puréed vegetables blended with liquid
- All fruit juices
- Cooked cereals
- Plain ice cream, sherbet, vanilla pudding, custard

THE SOFT, BLAND DIET

This is a menu that doctors and parents turn to almost instinctively when children get sick. The food is meant to be simple, soft in consistency, and easy to chew. Harsh fibers, strong spices, or highly flavored foods are to be avoided. When you are wondering what to serve a sick child, peruse this list and pick an item you think might be appealing.

■ **Bread, cereal, rice, and pasta group:**
White, fine whole-grain, or rye bread; cooked cornmeal, farina, hominy grits, or oatmeal; puffed rice, corn flakes, Rice Krispies; plain rice, pasta, and noodles; plain cake and cookies made without nuts

■ **Vegetable group:**
Cooked asparagus, beets, carrots, green and yellow wax beans, peas, spinach, winter squash, sweet and white potatoes. *Note:* raw or strongly flavored vegetables, such as broccoli, Brussels sprouts, cauliflower, and cucumber, should be avoided.

■ **Fruit group:**
Cooked or canned fruit, such as peaches, pears, and applesauce; ripe bananas or peeled ripe peaches and pears; any pure fruit juice products

■ **Milk, yogurt, and cheese group:**
Milk and milk-based drinks and soup made with allowed ingredients; American cheese, Swiss cheese, mild cheddar cheese, cottage cheese, and ricotta cheese; ice cream, pudding, and custard. *Note:* avoid any spicy cheeses or those with seeds or nuts.

■ **Meat, poultry, fish, dry beans, eggs, and nut group:**
Tender meat, poultry, and fish; any style of cooked egg except fried.
Note: fried or very fatty meats such as corned beef, cold

cuts, and frankfurters may not be well tolerated; neither may cooked dried beans or peanuts.

■ **Fats, oils, and sweets group:**
Butter, margarine, cream, cooking oils, sugar, jelly, gelatin, and hard candies

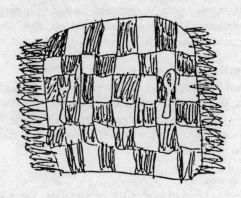

RECIPES

GRANDMA'S CHICKEN SOUP

YIELD: 8 1-CUP SERVINGS

Chicken soup is the traditional cure for colds, but it can also help settle sore tummies and it is the perfect transition food from liquids to solids. The ingredients carry essential nutrients and the warm, slightly salted liquid soothes the raspiest of throats.

> 3- to 4-lb. stewing chicken, rinsed and cut into pieces
> 2–3 quarts water
> 2 celery stalks with leaves
> 1 medium yellow onion, peeled
> 1/2 tsp. salt
> 1/4 tsp. pepper
> 1 carrot, scrubbed or peeled, and diced
> 1/2 cup diced celery
> 1 bay leaf
> 1 cup cooked curly noodles

1. In a large pot, combine the chicken, water, celery, onion, salt, and pepper. Bring to a boil. Lower the heat, cover pot, and let ingredients simmer for 2 hours.
2. Remove the chicken and set it aside to cool. Strain the broth. Return the strained broth to the soup pot and set aside.
3. Remove the chicken skin and discard it. Remove the chicken meat from the bone and cut into bite-sized pieces; set them aside.
4. Reheat the broth on medium heat. Add the carrots, celery, and bay leaf. Cook about 15 minutes or until carrots are

tender. Add the chicken and noodles. Stir and cook for 5 minutes to blend flavors. Season to taste—add a bit of salt or pepper if needed. Serve hot.

BASIC CHICKEN BROTH

YIELD: ABOUT 8 CUPS

1. To make a clear chicken broth, complete above steps through number 2.
2. Add the bay leaf to the strained broth and cook for 15 minutes. Adjust for seasoning and serve as needed.
3. Use the remaining cooked chicken to make a casserole or a chicken salad. Leftover broth can be frozen in 1-cup portions for use in future recipes.

CREAM OF TOMATO SOUP

YIELD: 8 SERVINGS

Try this recipe as a substitute for the canned version. It is not as quick as heating up ready-made soup, but it is tastier and more nutritious.

>   *2 cups fresh tomatoes, chopped*
>   *1 tbsp. onion, minced*
>   *1 tsp. sugar*
>   *2 tbsp. butter*
>   *2 tbsp. all-purpose flour*
>   *¹/₄ tsp. salt*
>   *4 cups whole milk, warm*

1. In a saucepan, cook the tomatoes with the onion and sugar for 15 minutes on low heat. Press the mixture through a strainer to remove skins and seeds. Set aside.
2. In a large saucepan, melt the butter. Stir in the flour to make a paste and cook for 2 minutes; do not burn. Stir in the warm milk. Cook mixture on medium high heat until it almost comes to a boil, stirring constantly. It will thicken slightly.
3. Stir in the cooked tomato mixture. Reduce heat to low and simmer soup for 10 minutes. Serve warm.

INDIVIDUAL CHICKEN POT PIE

YIELD: 4 1-CUP PIES

Chicken baked in a creamy sauce is very comforting. Freeze unused pies for use at another time.

> *3 tbsp. butter*
> *6 tbsp. all-purpose flour*
> *2 cups warm milk or chicken broth*
> *1 1/2 cups chicken, diced and cooked*
> *1 medium carrot, scrubbed, chopped, and cooked*
> *1 small onion, chopped (optional)*
> *1 ready-made pie crust*

1. Preheat the oven to 350°F. In a pot, melt the butter and stir in the flour to make a paste. Cook for 2 minutes on medium heat. Stir in the warm liquid (milk or chicken broth) and simmer for 5 minutes until the liquid becomes the consistency of cream. Add the chicken, carrots, and onion. Remove pot from heat and set aside.
2. Divide the pie crust into 8 even-sized pieces. Roll 4 of the pieces into circles about 6 in. in diameter. Line each of the 4 1-cup-capacity custard cups or miniature soufflé dishes with one of the pieces of the rolled dough.
3. Divide the chicken mixture equally among the 4 cups. Roll out the remaining 4 dough portions into 5-in. circles and use them to cover the top of each pie. Pierce a hole in each crust and bake for 30 minutes. Serve warm.

ROAST CHICKEN WITH GRAVY

YIELD: 6–8 SERVINGS

I have a vivid memory of traveling to New York City in the fourth grade to see the Westminster Dog Show at Madison Square Garden. Our family stayed at the glamorous Waldorf Astoria Hotel for 4 days. Unfortunately, the trip was marred by my upset tummy. To my satisfaction, my mother found us a cafeteria with simple roast chicken on the menu. It was the perfect antidote, and to this day, when anyone in my family has a stomachache, a lightly seasoned roast chicken goes in the oven.

For the roast chicken:
3- to 4-lb. roasting chicken
1 onion, peeled
Salt
Pepper

For the gravy:
1 1/2 cups water
1 bay leaf
Chicken neck and gizzard
2–3 tbsp. all-purpose flour
1/2 cup chicken broth (optional)

To make the roast chicken:
1. Preheat the oven to 325°F.
2. Remove the chicken neck and gizzard and set them aside, then rinse the poultry.
3. Season the cavity with salt and pepper and place the onion inside.
4. Roast the chicken for 90 minutes or until juices run clear when the skin is pricked with a fork. Serve hot with the chicken gravy and a side dish of potatoes or noodles.

To make the chicken gravy:

5. While the chicken cooks, simmer the neck and gizzard in a pot in 1 cup of the water, seasoned with a bay leaf. When the chicken is cooked, transfer it to a platter.
6. Skim the visible grease from the drippings in the roasting pan.
7. In a bowl, add 2–3 tbsp. all-purpose flour to the pan drippings and mix into a paste.
8. Remove the neck and gizzard from the pot. Strain the cooking water, put it back into the pot, and stir the flour and pan drippings into it. Cook on low heat until the gravy starts to thicken; add an additional ½ cup water or chicken broth if the gravy is too thick.

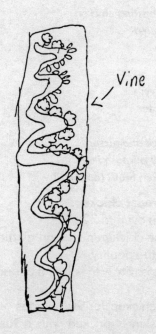

Vine

MERRY MEAT LOAF

YIELD: 4–6 SERVINGS

In our house, I always adorn the top of the loaf with a bit of catsup. Sometimes the catsup forms a smiling, merry face. I find this is just the right food on cold winter days or when appetites are small or tummies are tender.

> 1 lb. ground beef
> 2 large eggs
> 1 cup stale bread, torn into small pieces, or an equal amount of prepared bread crumbs or even dry, unsweetened breakfast cereal, like corn flakes
> 1 small onion, minced
> 2 tbsp. catsup
> ¹/₄ tsp. salt (optional)
> 1 tsp. dried parsley

1. Preheat oven to 350°F.
2. In a large bowl, combine all ingredients. Mix them with hands or a spoon until all ingredients are very well blended and evenly distributed.
3. Shape the meat into a loaf. Place it on a lightly oiled roasting pan—the type with slits in it. This will allow the grease to drip out of the meat. Cook meat for 1 hour or until it is no longer pink inside.

MACARONI AND CHEESE

YIELD: 4 SERVINGS

Because this dish is soft, creamy, and easy to chew, it makes a good sick-day food. Almost all kids like it, and it is even easy to prepare from scratch.

>*8 oz. elbow macaroni*
>*2 cups grated cheddar cheese*
>*¹/₂ tsp. prepared mustard (optional)*
>*1 ¹/₂ cups hot milk*

1. Preheat oven to 350°F.
2. Cook the elbow noodles according to the instructions on the label; do not overcook. Drain noodles and rinse them with hot water.
3. Lightly grease an oven-safe dish. Combine the cooked pasta with the cheese, mustard, and milk. Stir and bake for 30 minutes. If your child does not like a crispy crust, cover the top with aluminum foil while baking.

GRAND GRILLED-CHEESE SANDWICH

YIELD: 1 SANDWICH

The perfect sick-day grilled cheese is crustless and just ever so lightly browned, never burned! White sliced bread is usually the bread of choice, but a fresh Italian bread or a delicate white sourdough can be sublime, too. Fill the inside of the sandwich with the type of cheese your child likes best—or even combine 2 different favorite flavors for a change.

> *2 slices bread*
> *2 oz. sliced cheese—cheddar, American, Muenster, or Swiss*
> *1–2 tsp. butter*

1. Assemble the sandwich, trim the crusts, and butter the outside slices of bread.
2. Place the sandwich on a warm—not hot—grill, and cover it with a heavy lid. Keep a watchful eye so the bread does not burn.
3. Cut the sandwich on the diagonal or into 4 equal squares. Serve while still warm.

CINNAMON TOAST STICKS

YIELD: 1 SERVING

No one really needs a recipe for cinnamon toast; this is more of a variation to make it more appealing. This is truly a food for pampering your child, reserved for sick days and when spirits need lifting.

> *1 or 2 slices of white bread*
> *1 tbsp. butter, melted*
> *Sugar and cinnamon, about 1 tsp. each*
> *1 orange slice (optional)*

1. Toast the bread until ever so lightly browned.
2. Cut it into 3 or 4 even-sized sticks.
3. Dip one side of each stick in the melted butter, then into the sugar-cinnamon mixture.
4. Serve the sticks on a pretty plate with the cinnamon sides up. Garnish the plate with an orange slice.

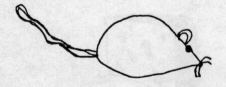

POTATOES

When nothing seems to appeal to your child, try preparing a baked potato. Its bland flavor and high digestibility make it a great sick-day food. It is, of course, easy to prepare and inexpensive, and it contains essential nutrients, such as fiber, vitamins, and energy-giving carbohydrates. Mashed and scalloped potatoes (recipes follow) can be real kid pleasers, too.

BAKED POTATOES

1. Idaho and russet potatoes make the best baked potatoes. Scrub them and then pierce the skin with a fork.
2. Bake at 350°F for 45 to 55 minutes or on high in the microwave oven for 3–4 minutes, depending on the size of the potatoes.

WHIPPED MASHED POTATOES

1. Peel 3 or 4 all-purpose potatoes and cook them whole in boiling salted water until tender when pierced with a fork. This takes 15–20 minutes, depending on the size of the potatoes.
2. Drain the water. Mash the potatoes with an electric mixer, adding enough butter and milk to make the mixture smooth.

SCALLOPED POTATOES

3 medium potatoes, peeled and sliced very thin
Salt and pepper
2 tbsp. all-purpose flour
3 tbsp. butter
1 cup milk

1. Preheat oven to 350°F.
2. Use half the potatoes to line the bottom of a buttered baking dish. Sprinkle with half the flour and dot with half the butter.
3. Layer the remaining potatoes on top and sprinkle with the remaining flour and butter.
4. Pour the milk over the potatoes and bake for 1½ hours. Serve warm.

WARM LIQUIDS

Most children today are not familiar with warm beverages other than hot cocoa or soup. For this reason, parents might overlook other warm fluids when their children are ill. A cup of warm liquid can soothe a scratchy throat, relieve a stuffed-up nose, and replenish essential lost fluids. They do need to be tailored to meet your child's taste preference: add a bit of honey, lemon, or cinnamon for flavor. Try the suggestions that follow and experiment with your own variations. Younger toddlers often don't like tea or even warm cider, but by age 3 or 4, many children find them more appealing. Some teas are credited with medicinal effects. Peppermint tea is said to settle a stomach-ache. Hyssop tea can soothe a mild throat irritation and loosen up phlegm. Chamomile is another favorite for easing tummy-aches, and tea made with ginger might ease motion sickness. Sample a variety of teas to find one your child likes and use it to make the Tea with Honey that follows.

TEA WITH HONEY

Whenever I had a sore throat, cough, or cold, my mother served cinnamon toast to help scratch an impossibly itchy throat and followed it with a cup of warm tea laced with golden honey. It seemed to help.

1. Simply brew a mild tea that your child likes.
2. Add a generous portion of golden honey. (Do not give honey to children under 1 year of age because of the risk of infant botulism.)
3. The cinnamon toast is optional, but a decorative teacup can certainly make the tea more elegant.

WARM CIDER

I add 1 tsp. sugar to this because my kids like it sweeter, and the addition of extra sugar almost guarantees that they will finish the whole thing and get the essential fluid the cider provides.

> *1 cup cider, apple juice, or cranberry apple juice*
> *1 tsp. brown sugar*

1. Combine the cider and the sugar.
2. Heat on the stovetop until sugar is dissolved. Serve warm.

MOCK TODDY

This recipe is adapted from my grown-up version of a hot toddy—minus the alcohol, of course.

> *6 oz. water*
> *2 tsp. brown sugar*
> *Dash of cinnamon*
> *1/4 tsp. lemon juice*

1. Combine all the ingredients and bring to a simmer.
2. Stir until sugar is dissolved. Serve warm, not hot.

FRUITY MILK SHAKES

YIELD: 1 SERVING

BANANA MILK SHAKE

This can make a good alternative to traditional breakfast foods. Use it on sick days when appetite is poor.

> *1 ripe banana*
> *1 cup cold milk*
> *1 tsp. vanilla*

1. In a blender, combine all the ingredients and purée until smooth.
2. Serve right away.

STRAWBERRY MILK SHAKE

YIELD: 1 SERVING

Strawberries are a great vitamin C source and a good way to get fiber.

> *1 cup strawberries, sliced and tops removed*
> *1 cup cold milk*
> *¹/₂ cup strawberry or vanilla ice cream*

1. Purée all ingredients in a blender until smooth.
2. Serve right away.

EGGNOG

YIELD: 1 SERVING

Because raw eggs carry a risk of salmonella poisoning, pasteurized egg substitutes are used in this eggnog recipe instead of fresh eggs. The egg substitute is still a good source of protein. Fresh eggs can be used. If you like hot eggnog, see the variation below.

>   *1 cup whole milk*
>   *1 tbsp. sugar*
>   *¼ cup egg substitute*

1. Purée all ingredients in the blender.
2. Serve over ice.

VARIATION: HOT EGGNOG

1. Combine the above ingredients in a saucepan, substituting a fresh egg for the egg substitute.
2. Turn the heat on medium and cook the eggnog until it almost comes to a boil, stirring all the while with an electric mixer on low speed. Continue stirring with the mixer and let the eggnog simmer for 1 minute without boiling it. The eggnog is done when it is hot and smooth.
3. If you like the flavor of vanilla stir in 1 tsp. before serving. Serve warm in a mug with freshly grated nutmeg.

RICE PUDDING

This is a slow-cooking dessert, perfect for times when you will be home for most of the day.

¹/₂ cup white rice
4 cups whole milk
¹/₂ tsp. cinnamon
¹/₂ tsp. nutmeg
¹/₂ cup white sugar
1 tsp. vanilla

1. Preheat the oven to 300°F.
2. In a bowl, combine all ingredients except the vanilla and mix well.
3. Lightly butter a 4-cup-capacity oven-safe dish, and pour the rice mixture into the dish.
4. Set it in a pan of hot water and bake for 3 hours. Stir at least twice in the first hour of baking. In the last hour of baking, stir in the vanilla.
5. When the pudding is done, most of the milk should be absorbed and the rice will be tender.
6. Serve warm or cold. Top with cold ice cream or vanilla yogurt if desired.

INDIVIDUAL BAKED CUSTARD

YIELD: 1 SERVING

The combination of milk and egg makes this a very rich protein source. Serve it as a meal replacement, a snack, or even for breakfast. This recipe can be doubled or tripled if necessary.

1 large egg
4 tsp. sugar
1 cup scalded milk
¹/₄ tsp. milk
Nutmeg, freshly grated (optional)

1. Combine all ingredients except the nutmeg in a bowl and mix well.
2. Pour into a 1-cup custard dish and sprinkle with nutmeg if desired.
3. Place in a pan of water and bake for 30 minutes or until the custard is set. You can tell it is cooked when a knife inserted comes out clean. Serve warm or cold.

VANILLA PUDDING

YIELD: 4 SERVINGS

The store-bought version might be quicker, but it is not better tasting. Try the chocolate variation below for a change in taste.

⅓ cup sugar
3 tbsp. cornstarch
2 cups whole milk, warm
1 tsp. vanilla
1 tsp. butter

1. Sift together the sugar and cornstarch and set the mixture aside.
2. Heat the milk in a saucepan on medium heat. Gradually stir in the sugar mixture, stirring constantly until the mixture starts to thicken. Stir in the vanilla and butter.
3. Pour into 4 individual cups or 1 bowl, refrigerate, and serve when cold. To prevent a skin from forming, cover the bowl top with plastic wrap before refrigerating.
4. To make chocolate pudding, melt a 1-oz. square of unsweetened chocolate in the milk before adding the sugar mixture, then proceed as directed above.

CHUNKY APPLESAUCE

Homemade applesauce is easy and economical, particularly in the fall when apples are in abundance. Cooking brings out the sweetness in fruit. Sugar is omitted from this recipe, but if the apples you use are tart, add 1 tsp. of sugar. Cortland apples make good applesauce, but in our house, we often use a variety of apples—even Golden Delicious and green Granny Smiths. Serve it as a dessert, side dish, or at breakfast. Most kids find apples to be very easy on the tummy and they are a good source of fiber.

4 cups apples, peeled, cored, and chopped
1 tsp. lemon
$^1/_2$ tsp. cinnamon
$^1/_4$ tsp. grated nutmeg

1. In a large saucepan, combine all the ingredients plus $^1/_4$ cup water. Cover and simmer for 10 minutes or until apples are soft.
2. Mash the cooked apples with a fork, or for a smooth sauce, press the cooked apples through a sieve or a food mill.

GINGERBREAD CAKE

YIELD: 1 CAKE, 8″ × 8″

Ginger is said to calm and ease a queasy stomach. This cake is so good don't just serve it when sick. It makes a good after school snack and a wonderful treat when served warm, topped with a bit of ice cream or fresh whipped cream.

¹/₄ cup butter, softened
¹/₄ cup brown sugar
1 large egg
1¹/₂ cups all-purpose flour
1 tsp. cinnamon
¹/₄ tsp. ground cloves
¹/₄ tsp. ground nutmeg
1 tbsp. ginger
1 tsp. baking soda
¹/₂ cup molasses combined with ¹/₂ cup boiling water

1. Preheat the oven to 350°F.
2. In a bowl, cream the butter and the sugar until smooth. Add the egg and blend well.
3. In another bowl, combine all the dry ingredients.
4. Add the dry ingredients to the creamed butter, alternating with the molasses mixture, stirring until smooth. Do not overmix.
5. Pour batter into an 8-in.-square cake pan. Bake 20 minutes or until a knife comes out clean when inserted.

RAINBOW CAKE

YIELD: 1 CAKE, 8″ × 11″

A fresh slice of cake is a wonderful treat for a sick child, but frosting made with butter or shortening can be too rich for upset tummies. Try this version that uses only colorful sprinkles for a topping. The kids love it and don't miss the frosting at all.

¹/₄ cup softened butter
³/₄ cups sugar
2 eggs
1³/₄ cups all-purpose flour
¹/₄ tsp. salt
1 tbsp. baking powder
1 cup milk
1 tsp. vanilla
¹/₂ cup Rainbow Jimmies

1. In a bowl, cream together the sugar and butter until smooth. Beat in the egg.
2. In another bowl, combine all dry ingredients.
3. Add the flour to the butter mixture, alternating with the milk, until well blended. Stir in the vanilla.
4. Pour into an 8″ × 11″ lightly greased brownie pan. Sprinkle with the Jimmies and bake for 25 minutes.

HANSEL AND GRETEL PUDDING

YIELD: 8 SERVINGS

Instead of scattering stale bits of bread to feed the birds or mark trails like Hansel and Gretel, use it to make creamy, nourishing pudding. Here is a basic version with three scrumptious variations. All incorporate eggs and milk, protein-rich ingredients essential to any child's recovery. For an elegant touch, try the Meringue Topping listed below.

> *3 cups stale white bread, torn into cubes*
> *3 cups milk*
> *3 large eggs*
> *1/2 cup sugar*
> *1 tsp. vanilla*
> *1 tsp. cinnamon*
> *1/2 tsp. fresh nutmeg*

1. Preheat the oven to 350°F.
2. Place the bread in a lightly buttered casserole or soufflé dish.
3. In a separate bowl, beat together the eggs, milk, and flavorings.
4. Pour the milk mixture over the bread and let sit for 15 minutes.
5. Stir once, then bake for 45 minutes. The pudding should be dry and golden on top but soft and moist inside.
6. Serve with fresh whipped cream or cold vanilla ice cream.

MERINGUE TOPPING

1. Follow the directions above through step 2, but separate the eggs; combine only the yolks with the milk, then proceed with step 4 above.

2. Beat the egg whites with 3 tbsp. sugar until very stiff.
3. In the last 10 minutes of cooking, spread the meringue on top of the pudding and continue baking. The top will be golden brown when done. Use this topping on any of the following variations.

BANANA BREAD PUDDING

1. Substitute leftover slices of banana bread for the stale bread.
2. Reduce the sugar to ⅓ cup and follow the directions as described above.

GINGERBREAD PUDDING

1. Substitute leftover gingerbread cake for some or all of the white bread.
2. Reduce the sugar to ⅓ cup and bake as described above.

CHOCOLATE BREAD PUDDING

1. Melt 2 oz. unsweetened chocolate and set aside to cool slightly.
2. Blend the cooled chocolate with the eggs and milk.
3. Pour this chocolate mixture over the bread and soak as described above, then bake as directed.

5

QUESTIONS AND
ANSWERS

Not all questions about nutrition fit into the preceding chapters. Friends, neighbors, clients, and even family members ask me about many food-related issues. The questions that came up most often have been included in this section because they may apply to your child, too.

Q: What can I do when my 4-year-old refuses to eat? I am worried he is not getting the nutrition he needs.

A: Hunger strikes are not uncommon in preschool-aged children and, like you, most parents become alarmed by them. If your child is growing normally and is in general good health, you probably have nothing to worry about. In most cases, kids just are not hungry and will make up for what is missed at one meal by eating more the next. However, try to determine if the lack of interest is linked to an underlying cause. Is your child sick? Is he upset or nervous about something? Even going to visit at a new friend's house, though fun, can be a source of stress. Is there stress at the dinner table—arguments or fighting among siblings that can distract from eating? Is your child allowed to play with toys at the table or watch TV while eating?

Ask yourself if your meal schedule contributes to undereating. For example, has your child had a protein-rich snack, such as cheese or peanut butter, or a very sweet snack, such as a fruit drink, before a meal? These foods can dull an appetite. Are you expecting him to eat too much? Children need to eat child-sized, not adult-sized, portions.

You should never try to force your child to eat. Your responsibility is to provide good-tasting, nourishing food in a pleasant environment. It is then your child's responsibility to eat it when he is hungry. Here are some practical strategies to overcome or prevent hunger strikes:

- Establish a regular meal and snack schedule. Three meals plus two between-meal snacks works for most children between 1 and 10 years old.
- Snacks should precede meals by at least 45 minutes. If your child is clamoring for something to eat right before supper, give him an item that is meant to be served with dinner, such as a slice of bread, a carrot stick, or sliced tomato.
- Do not become a short-order cook. If your child is getting into the pattern of refusing meals and asking for something to eat 20 minutes later, inform him of the developing pattern. Reserve something from the prepared meal and offer that when a food request is made. Soon your child will realize that skipped meals will not result in specially prepared food items. Of course, this does not apply on true sick days!
- Eliminate distractions; no toys, books or games at the table.
- Talk to your child about eating. For some kids food is a source of control; not eating may be a way to get attention from Mom and Dad. Don't be angry with them; you can't blame them for wanting more time from the people they love the most. Try giving atten-

tion in a more positive way, like reading before a meal or involving your children in meal preparation and table setting. Then congratulate them when they do a nice job.

▪ In most cases refusing meals is temporary, but if it continues for more than two days, talk to your pediatrician.

Q: Everyone seems to think milk is such an important food, but my child doesn't like it. Should I be worried about her health?

A: Children do not need to drink milk, but they *do* need calcium, and milk is a superb calcium source. Fortunately, calcium can come from a lot of other dairy foods, such as cheese, yogurt, cream soup, and puddings made with milk; ice cream; and ice milk. Baked foods, such as muffins and quick breads made with milk, will contain some calcium. Nondairy calcium sources include leafy greens, broccoli, tofu, and beans. If your child does not drink milk, substitute with other dairy foods or calcium-rich vegetables and beans. If these are refused or can't be tolerated, a calcium supplement may be needed. Discuss this with your pediatrician.

Q: Everyone knows vegetables are important to children, but I don't think mine eat the recommended amounts. They just don't seem to like them. Is this serious?

A: First of all, don't give up on vegetables. Set a good example by eating them yourself. Vegetables are important because they carry minerals, fiber, and health-promoting chemicals. Adults who eat vegetables daily as part of a balanced diet have fewer illnesses. The effort to get your children to eat vegetables, then, is a worthwhile one, but don't be a fanatic. Offer a variety and ask your children how they like them prepared: cold, cooked, raw with a dip, or part of a stir fry. Try to accommodate these requests when it's practical. As the study mentioned in Chapter 1 suggests, repeatedly offering vegetables eventually results in their being eaten. In our family, we aim to serve two vegetables at meals. One of these is usually one of the children's favorites, but we always ask them to at least try a sample of the other even when they have tried it before and not liked it. You can also incorporate vegetables, such as zucchini, into muffins or serve them in soup or grate them into casseroles. I don't recommend "sneaking" them into food, because then your children will get into the game of Where Did Mommy Hide the Vegetables? and they will be suspicious of everything you cook. I suggest you be straightforward with your children: tell them that you believe vegetables are good for their health and will help them to keep healthy their whole life. A 2-year-old might not appreciate your honesty but your 8-year-old will have trouble invalidating that argument.

Q: I am worried about my baby. She is 10 months old and looks to me to be overweight when I compare her to other babies her age. Will she grow up to be fat?

A: An infant's "fatness" is related more to how much weight Mom gained while pregnant than to how fat the infant will be when older. How tall a baby is or how much she weighs in her first 2 years of life is not a predictor of her stature when older. Feed your baby following your pediatrician's guidelines and the recommendations suggested in Chapter 1. Do not start your child on a restricted or low-fat diet at this early age. Provide her with adequate breast milk or formula feedings and introduce a variety of appropriate foods, and let her appetite determine what she needs.

Q: Over the past few months, I have noticed that my 9-year-old really looks chubby. I do not want to start her on a diet, but I worry about her trend toward weight gain.

A: Good for you for not starting your daughter on a "diet." Too many young girls become obsessed with their weight by the time they reach adolescence. This obsession is created by the media, but families can make it worse. It is essential that parents not contribute to the problem by telling their children they need to lose weight. Little girls can interpret this as meaning they need to be fixed, which can lower their self-esteem, distort their body image, and begin a very unrewarding cycle of weight loss and calorie counting.

Obesity in our children is a serious matter that is getting worse. One out of five teens is now overweight; in the 1970s, the ratio was one in seven. Dieting is not the answer. Instead, focus on the factors causing the weight gain. If your child is gaining more weight than is appropriate for her height, she is eating more than she needs and is not exercising enough.

What to do about gradual weight gain:

■ Make it a family issue. Use the Food Guide Pyramid in Chapter 1 (see page 16). Have the whole family keep a diary for 3 days. Identify the food groups that are being over- or underconsumed. Look at the amount of foods that are a source of fat and sugar. What type of snack foods are being consumed? Children commonly consume more fruit drinks or even milk than they need. Remember, most juices and juice drinks carry the same number of calories as soda. Are enough fruits and vegetables being consumed, or are higher-calorie snack foods replacing them? Identify the trouble spots and then as a family make a plan to eat healthier.

■ How much TV does your child watch? Children who watch TV every day are fatter than those who do not. This is because they are less active and TV promotes the eating of high-fat, high-calorie foods. The average child watches 3 hours of TV per day. Consider eliminating TV during the week. Tape favorite shows if your child is desperate to see them. One friend of mine with a 10-year-old daughter and an 8-year-old son did this, and after several weeks of the new rule, her daughter confessed she actually liked it because she no longer had to arrange her school and social life around TV shows. Children will be more creative and physically active when the TV is off. Try it— you'll see!

■ Encourage exercise. Take a walk or a bike ride. Buy the sound track to your child's favorite movies and encourage dancing. My 6- and 7-year-old will dance for an hour or more to the *Lion King* songs, and they really work up a sweat.

Q: I am returning to work after giving birth to my first child and I am worried about his getting sick at day care. Is day care unhealthy for my infant?

A: A 1993 article by Dr. Giebink in the *Journal of Pediatrics* included a study that compared the health of children in day care and in group home care to that of children exclusively cared for at home. It showed that the children in the group home or day-care centers had significantly more respiratory and ear infections than the children who were cared for in their own home. None of the children in the study ever required hospitalization for treatment, but 21 percent of the children in center care required implantation of ear tubes for recurrent ear infections, while only 3 percent in home care needed tubes. In the children's second and third years of life, the magnitude of difference in illness rates decreased between children in group care and those in home care.

Children experience a lot of mild illness when they are very young, but group care does seem to accelerate the rate, at least during the youngest years. If at all possible, try to arrange for home care for your baby's first year of life.

Q: Both my husband and I work full time and we must rely on day care. When are our kids too sick to go to day care?

A: Just recently, the AAP and the American Public Health Department collaborated to develop national health and safety guidelines to answer this question. In most cases, children with mild illness do not need to be excluded from care as long as the illness does not affect participation in usual activities or require more care from the staff. Most centers will not have enough staff to attend to a truly sick child (as defined below). If the child has an illness that can be transmitted to other children, he should be kept at home, but many children are not symptomatic when they are actually contagious. Keep your child home if he has a fever, uncontrolled diarrhea, vomiting, persistent abdominal pain (more than 2 hours), a rash with fever, or conjunctivitis. Ask your doctor for additional guidelines.

Q: When I know my child is too sick to go to day care, what should I do?

A: The value of having an attentive parent or close relative care for a sick child cannot be underestimated. If at all possible, try to stay home with your child when she is truly sick. Arrange with your partner to share sick-day responsibilities. If you have family close at hand, ask for their help. A friendly, loving face can help a child really get the rest and comfort she needs when ill.

Many day-care centers can provide care in a "get well" room if the illness is mild; this has the advantage of causing the least amount of disruption to the child and family. When your child is sick, send her with special sick-day items; include her favorite blanket, book, or toy. Inform the day-care staff that your child needs extra care and tell them what she likes. If she is an older child, send her with a tape player and cassettes of favorite stories or even a tape of you reading a story. Make one up ahead of time. Send in a happy family photo that she can peek at when she's sad. Call during the day to see how she is and even arrange for a person-to-person chat if possible. Children like to talk on the phone. Even though they don't say much on the phone when they're young, it must be reassuring to hear Mommy or Daddy's voice.

In some cases your community may have professionals who will care for your child in your home when she is sick. Check this out long before your child becomes ill. The disadvantage to this alternative is that if the care giver is a stranger, this may stress your child even more—and it is very expensive. If you need help locating care for your sick child, ask your pediatrician's office about any local sick-day care providers. Or, try calling Child Care Aware at (800) 424-2246; this is a nationwide network for child-care referrals, including sick care. Again, arrange sick-day backup before you need it. If care will be provided in an unfamiliar location, make sure you visit the place and meet the care giver before you use the service.

Q: Are fast-food restaurants really bad? My children love them and I don't have to worry about their making too much noise or my spending too much money.

A: Fast-food restaurants are not all bad. For the reasons you mentioned, parents find them a true alternative to cooking at home. However, if you frequent them a lot, you will have trouble selecting a healthy diet because most of the items served are high in fat, and fruits and vegetables are just not on most menus.

There is no cast-in-stone recommended dietary allowance for fat, but in general, 65 grams per day is likely to meet the needs of any child over age 4. Divided among three meals and two snacks, that equals 13 grams at each meal or snack. A cheeseburger, small order of fries, and a milk shake carry about 32 grams of fat, or about half the fat your child needs for the whole day. If that cheeseburger is replaced by a McDonald's Big Mac, add another 15 grams of fat, for a total of 45 grams.

Besides the fat content problem, there is the lack of fruits and vegetables—the foods that can protect your child from illness and disease. Though potatoes are part of the vegetable group, when they are fried and heavily processed they can no longer compare nutritionally with their original form.

For better or worse, fast-food restaurants are here to stay. If you want to keep your children well nourished, you must learn to navigate the menu:

▪ If you eat at a fast-food restaurant occasionally, consider it a treat and let your children have what they like.
▪ If you eat at a fast-food restaurant weekly, start looking at it as an extension of the nutrition values you try to follow at home. The best choices are the plain, unadorned hamburgers. Avoid the deluxe, jumbo, or double-burger products. These are dripping with high-fat sauces and excessive meat portions. Most chicken and fish sandwiches are fried or served with high-fat sauces. McDonald's McGrilled Chicken Classic is a good low-fat exception (3 grams per serving). Side salads are a good choice, but use only small

amounts of the dressing provided. All French fries carry 10 to 20 grams of fat, depending on the serving size, so try sharing servings among the family instead of everybody getting their own. Low-fat milks and fruit juices are good drinks to choose. Skip the colas and milk shakes, except as a treat, and avoid diet sodas because, though they don't carry sugar, they replace more nutritious drinks.

▪ If fast-food meals are a part of your children's regular eating pattern, be rigorous about what they are eating for snacks and school lunches and while at friends' houses. Somewhere during the day, fruits, vegetables, and low-fat dairy foods need to find a place in your children's menu.

Q: My baby is 5 months old and still cries more than most babies his age. My doctor says he is fine. Is there anything that can help?

A: The natural progression of crying is that it will improve with time. For the family enduring the howls of the new family member, it is so stressful that help is hoped for sooner rather than later. Medication, dietary changes, alteration in stimulation, and change in the parent–infant interaction are often looked to for relief, but not always with success. The medication once used to treat crying (dicyclomine) is no longer prescribed for fear it will cause respiratory side effects. Dietary changes, such as removing cow's milk from the diet, help in only a small number of cases. Responding to crying with more stimulation, such as carrying or giving toys, may actually make the problem worse. What does seem to be useful are changes in caretaking behavior.

In a 1994 study conducted in England, trained counselors conducted in-depth interviews with parents of babies who cried for as much as 6 hours per day. Based on the information gained from the counselors, parents were given recommendations on changing their own behavior to alleviate the crying. Recommended changes included establishing a clear daily routine for eating, sleeping, outings, and playtime. Overstimulation, such as frequent rocking or carrying, was reduced when appropriate and adding stimulation was recommended when indicated. Feeding babies when they cry or until they fall asleep or taking babies on car rides to make them sleepy were discouraged because they did not foster the babies' ability to develop self-control. Parents were also asked to become aware of a distinction between cries for food, cries of discomfort, and cries of fear or frustration. Parents were instructed not to immediately intervene when their babies cry, unless the cries were out of pain or fear. Unfortunately, there is no one simple remedy that works for all families. You will have to identify the behaviors in your household that might contribute to crying. Contacting a mental-health therapist trained in family therapy may be useful in gaining assistance in identifying behavior that contributes to your baby's need to cry.

Q: Several of my friends use homeopathic treatments when their children get sick. Are alternative medical treatments safe for children?

A: Results of a recent study show that of the more than 100 forms of alternative medical therapies, most parents choose one of four treatments for their children: chiropractic, homeopathy, naturopathy, and acupuncture. Parents who turn to alternative medicine are often users themselves and choose alternative medicine when their children suffer from a chronic condition. Repeat ear infections are commonly cited as a reason for seeking alternative care. This study's results showed that parents do not abandon their pediatrician or conventional medicine; instead, alternative medicine is used as a parallel form of treatment.

The safety of alternative medicine depends on the therapy and the therapist. Many conventional medical practitioners are concerned about alternative medical treatments for fear they will do harm or mask or not identify a serious underlying condition. It is your responsibility to be sure your child is getting adequate medical care. If you treat your child with alternative medical treatments, consider these points:

■ Be wary of any practitioner who offers a cure when no one else can.
■ Keep your pediatrician informed of your treatment choices.
■ If the treatment is not effective, treatment should be sought elsewhere, because a practitioner treating only symptoms may miss underlying disease.

Q: Is herbal therapy safe for children?

A: Herbal products are not well regulated, and not all herbs are benign—some are capable of causing serious side effects. Because children have smaller bodies, the risk of harmful side effects may be greater for them; a dose safe for grownups could be harmful to children. In Europe, medicinal herbs are carefully regulated and must conform to standards of efficacy and safety. Such standards would be of a benefit to children and adults alike in the United States. For now, parents practicing herbal therapy should proceed with caution. The safety and efficacy of herbal therapy remains unestablished.

Q: I learned helpful relaxation techniques in my childbirth preparation classes. I still use them when I get really tense. Can children be taught relaxation therapy, too?

A: I have not read any studies about relaxation therapy in children, but in our house we have used controlled breathing to ease tummy-aches and progressive muscle relaxation to assist my 5-year-old on sleepless nights.

It was Herbert Benson, M.D., of Harvard Medical School, who brought relaxation therapy out of the realm of mysticism and into the lexicon of mainstream medicine. Many books based on Dr. Benson's work can be found in the libraries and bookstores around the country. His four basic principles, which can also be used with children, include the following: (1) establish a mental focal point, (2) have a passive attitude, (3) be situated in a comfortable position, and (4) be in a quiet environment.

I have asked my children to use breathing as their mental focal point. I have them lie down in their bed and get comfortable. I tell them to become aware of their breathing and to think of nothing else but their breathing. I ask them to inhale comfortably and imagine they are sending their breath deep into their tummy, then exhale slowly and quietly. I then repeat that message several times, using a quiet, steady voice.

Another relaxation technique that can be very helpful in the treatment of headaches is known as progressive muscle relaxation. With this technique, each major group of muscles is individually tensed, then released. When all the muscles have been tensed and then released, from the toes to the forehead, a very comfortable sense of relaxation can occur. Don't be surprised if you get a few giggles from your child, but that is good, too, because laughing is a great stress reliever.

Ask your child to lie down in a comfortable, quiet spot. Tell him to think of something quiet but pleasant, such as a colorful butterfly or a sleeping family of kittens. Then, starting at his toes, ask your child to squeeze the muscles in his toes, one foot at a time, as tightly as he can and hold the tension for a few seconds, then release. Help him work his way through his foot, then his other foot, and up both legs to his stomach, fingers, arms—all the way to his head, nose, even forehead.

The first time I tried the breathing relaxation technique with my daughter Emily, it was very effective at relieving a stomachache that I strongly suspected was due to nerves. These techniques are both harmless and potentially very beneficial. They also reinforce the concept that healing can come from within and not exclusively through medical intervention.

RESOURCES

The following are additional sources of information about nutrition and children's health.

ORGANIZATIONS

American Academy of Pediatrics
141 Northwest Point Road
P.O. Box 927
Elk Grove Village, IL 60007

American Dietetic Association
216 W. Jackson Boulevard, Suite 800
Chicago, IL 60606-6995

ADA Nutrition Hotline
(800) 366-1655

Parents Anonymous
(800) 882-1250

RECOMMENDED HEALTH
AND NUTRITION NEWSLETTERS

Nutrition Action Health Letter
Center for Science in the Public Interest
1875 Connecticut Avenue N.W., Suite 300
Washington, D.C. 20009-5728
($19.95 for 12 issues)

Tufts University Diet and Nutrition Letter
New subscription information
P.O. Box 57857
Boulder, CO 80322-7857
($19.95 for 12 issues)

Vegetarian Times
1140 Lake Street
Oak Park, IL 60301
(312) 848-8100

The University of California Wellness Letter
P.O. Box 420148
Palm Coast, FL 32142
($20.00 for 12 issues)

SELECTED BIBLIOGRAPHY

Most of the information in this book regarding nutrition and illness in children, its treatment, and its prognosis is taken from the textbooks listed below. In addition to these references, specific articles that may be of interest to the reader are also listed here under the chapter that discusses the particular topic.

American Academy of Pediatrics, Committee on Nutrition. *Pediatric Nutrition Handbook*. 3rd ed. American Academy of Pediatrics, Elk Grove Village, IL, 1993.

Aspen Reference Group, Sara Neil Di Lima, senior editor. *Dietitian's Patient Education Manual*. Aspen Publications, Gaithersburg, MD, 1994.

Boston Children's Hospital. *The New Child Health Encyclopedia*. Dell Publishing, New York, 1987.

Graef, John W., M.D. *Manual of Pediatric Therapeutics*. 5th ed. Little, Brown, Boston, 1993.

Goodhart, R. S. *Modern Nutrition in Health and Disease*. 8th ed. Lea & Febiger, Philadelphia, 1993.

Hathaway, William E., M.D. *Current Pediatric Diagnosis and Treatment*. 11th ed. Appleton & Lange, Norwalk, CT, 1994.

Merenstein, Gerald B., M.D., FAAP (ed.). *Handbook of Pediatrics* 17th ed. Appleton & Lange, Norwalk, CT, 1994.

National Research Council, Subcommittee on the Tenth Edition of the RDAs. *Recommended Dietary Allowances*. 10th ed. National Academy Press, National Research Council, 1989.

Wong, Donna L. *Clinical Manual of Pediatric Nursing.* 3rd ed., CV Mosby, St. Louis, MO, 1990.

CHAPTER 1

Achterberg, C. A. "How to Put the Food Guide Pyramid in Practice." *Journal of the American Dietetic Association.* September: 94:1030–1035, 1994.

Birch, L. "The Variability of Young Children's Energy Intake." *New England Journal of Medicine* 324:232–235, 1991.

Committee on Nutrition. "The Use of Whole Cow's Milk in Infancy." *Pediatrics* June:1105–1109, 1992.

American Academy of Pediatrics Work Group on Cow's Milk Protein and Diabetes Mellitus. "Infant Feeding Practices and Their Possible Relationships to the Etiology of Diabetes Mellitus." *Pediatrics* November 94:752–754, 1994.

Johnson, R. K. "Characterizing Nutrient Intake of Children by Sociodemographic Factors." *Public Health Reports* May/June 109:414–420, 1994.

Johnson, R. K. "Maternal Employment and the Quality of Young Children's Diets: Empirical Evidence Based on the 1987–1988 Nationwide Food Consumption Survey." *Pediatrics* August 90:245–249, 1992.

Klesges, R. C. "Effects of Television on Metabolism: Potential Implications for Childhood Obesity." *Pediatrics* 91:81–83, 1993.

National Research Council, Committee on Pesticides in the Diets of Infants and Children. *Pesticides in the Diets of Infants and Children.* National Academy Press, Washington, D.C., 1993.

Pinnock, C. B. "Relationship Between Milk Intake and Mucus Production in Adult Volunteers Challenged with Rhinovirus-2." *American Review of Respiratory Disease* 141:352–356, 1990.

Shea, S. "Variability and Self-Regulation of Energy Intake in Young Children in Their Everyday Environment." *Pediatrics* October 90:542–546, 1992.

Sullivan, S. A. "Infant Dietary Experience and Acceptance of Solid Foods." *Pediatrics* February 93:271–277, 1994.

CHAPTER 2

French, G. M. "Blowing Away Shot Pain: A Technique for Pain Management During Immunization." *Pediatrics* 384–388, 1994.

CHAPTER 3

ASTHMA

"Fish Oils Shown to Reduce Asthma Risk." *USA Today,* May 23, 1995.

Middleton, Elliott, Jr. (ed.). *Allergy Principles and Practice,* 4th ed. pp. 1236, 1240–1241, 1255–1256, 1597, 1690–1691. CV Mosby, St. Louis, MO, 1993.

"Salt and Asthma." Nutrition Action Health Letter 21:4, 1994.

BEDWETTING

Rappaport, L. "The Treatment of Nocturnal Enuresis—Where Are We Now?" (Commentary.) *Pediatrics* 92:465–466, 1993.

CHOLESTEROL

"Cholesterol in Children: Healthy Eating Is a Family Affair. Parents' Guide." National Institutes of Health, NIH Pub. No. 92-3099, November 1992.

Dennison, B. A. "Challenges to Implementing the Current Pediatric Cholesterol Screening Guidelines into Practice." *Pediatrics* September: 94:296–302, 1994.

Shea, Steven. "Is There a Relationship Between Dietary Fat and Stature or Growth in Children Three to Five Years of Age?" *Pediatrics* October: 92:579–586, 1993.

Wong, N. D. "Television Viewing and Pediatric Hypercholesterolemia." *Pediatrics* July: 90:75–79, 1992.

COLDS

Schardt, B. "Grading Vitamin C." *Nutrition Action Healthletter* November, pp. 10–11, 1994.

COLD SORES

"Myth of the Month: Lysine for Herpes." *Nutrition and the MD*
April: 10:4, 1984.

COLIC

Parkin, P. C. "Passage of Time Remains the Best Cure for Colic."
Pediatrics August: 92:9, 1993.

CONSTIPATION

McClung, H. J. "Is Combination Therapy for Encopresis Nutritionally Safe?" *Pediatrics* March: 91:591–594, 1993.

Williams, C. L. "Importance of Dietary Fiber in Childhood." *Journal of the American Dietetics Assoc.* 95:1140–1146, 1995.

DIARRHEA

Brown, K. H. "Nonhuman Milks in the Dietary Management of
Young Children with Acute Diarrhea: A Meta-analysis of Clinical Trials." *Pediatrics* January: 93:17–27, 1994.

Smith, M. E. "Carbohydrate Absorption from Fruit Juice in Young
Children." *Pediatrics* March: 95:340–344, 1995.

EAR INFECTIONS

Williams, R. D. "Protecting Little Pitchers' Ears." *FDA Consumer*
December: 12:10–14, 1994.

Duncan, B. "Exclusive Breast-Feeding for at Least Four Months
Protects Against Otitis Media." *Pediatrics* May: 91:867–872,
1993.

"Otitis Media with Effusion in Young Children, Clinical Practice
Guideline." Agency for Health Care Policy and Research,
AHCPR Pub. No. 94-0622, July 1994.

FOOD ALLERGY

Anderson, J. A. "Tips When Considering the Diagnosis of Food
Allergy." *Topics in Clinical Nutrition* 9:11–21, 1994.

HaHevig, S. N. "Maternal Avoidance of Eggs, Cow's Milk, and Fish
During Lactation: Effect on Allergenic Manifestations, Skin-
Prick Tests, and Specific IgE Antibody in Children at Age Four
Years." *Pediatrics* 89:735–739, 1992.

Kendall, P. A. "Managing Food Allergies and Sensitivities." *Topics in Clinical Nutrition* 9:1–10, 1994.

Perkin, J. E. "Update on Food Allergy Research." *Topics in Clinical Nutrition* 9:11:22–32, 1994.

HYPERACTIVITY

Accarrdo, P. "Nutrition and Behavior—the Legend Continues." *Pediatrics* January: 93:127–128, 1994.

Shaywitz, B. A. "Aspartame, Behavior and Cognitive Function in Children with Attention Deficit Disorder." *Pediatrics* January: 93:70–75, 1994.

Wender, E. H. "The Food Additive-Free Diet in the Treatment of Behavior Disorders. A review." *Journal of Developmental and Behavioral Pediatrics* February: 7:35–42, 1986.

IRON-DEFICIENCY ANEMIA

Walter T. "Effectiveness of Iron Fortified Infant Cereal in Prevention of Iron Deficiency Anemia." *Pediatrics* May: 91:976–982, 1993.

LEAD POISONING

Schaffer, S. "Lead Poisoning Risk Determination in an Urban Population Through the Use of a Standardized Questionnaire." *Pediatrics* February: 93:159–163, 1994.

Shannon, M. "Lead Intoxication from Lead-Contaminated Water Used to Reconstitute Infant Formula." *Clinical Pediatrics* 28:380–382, 1989.

"Preventing Lead Poisoning in Young Children—A Statement by the Centers for Disease Control." pp. 96–105. U.S. Government Printing Office, Washington, D.C., October, 1991.

SLEEP

Pinella, T. "Help Me Make It Through the Night: Behavioral Entrainment of Breastfed Infants' Sleep Patterns." *Pediatrics* February: 91:436–444, 1993.

Walker, M. "Sleep Feeding and Opinions." (Letter to the editor.) *Pediatrics* December: 9:883–885, 1993.

CHAPTER 5

Giebink, G. S. "Care of the Ill Child in Day-Care Settings." *Pediatrics* January: 91:229–233, 1993.

Jacobs, J. "Treatment of Acute Diarrhea with Homeopathic Medicine: A Randomized Clinical Trial in Nicaragua." *Pediatrics* May: 93:719–725, 1994.

Parkin, P. C. "Randomized Controlled Trial of Three Interventions in the Management of Persistent Crying of Infancy." *Pediatrics* August: 92:197–201, 1993.

Spigelblatt, L. "The Use of Alternative Medicine by Children." *Pediatrics* December: 94:811–814, 1994.

Wolke, D. "Excessive Infant Crying: A Controlled Study of Mothers Helping Mothers." *Pediatrics* September: 94:322–332, 1994.

RECIPE INDEX

The recipes in this book have been created with children in mind. They are not too fancy, too spicy, or exotic. Use this recipe index to locate all the foods that may appeal to your child.

SNACKS

Alphabet Sticks, 112
Buttermilk Banana Bread, 80
Cinnamon Toast Sticks, 240
Cucumber Boats, 65
Dr. Boodish's Never-Fail
   Constipation Recipe, 113
Dream Bean Dip, 109
Fruit 'n' Nuts, 63

Hearty Oatmeal Bread, 159
Honey and 'Jamas, 56
Plum and Yogurt Parfait, 131
Pretzel Rings, 219
South-of-the-Border Salsa, 51
Swiss Potatoes, 66
Teething Biscuits, 218

SOUP

ABC Soup, 141
Barley Soup, 123
Basic Chicken Broth, 232
Cream of Tomato Soup, 233
Fog Soup, 91

Grandma's Chicken Soup, 231
Lace Soup, 142
Sweet Garlic Soup, 88
Very Vegetable Soup, 214

DESSERTS

GENERAL INDEX

ABOUT THE AUTHOR

Eileen Behan is a member of the American Dietetic Association, a registered dietitian, and a mother of two. She holds a degree in home economics from Rivier College in Nashua, New Hampshire, and completed a traineeship in nutrition at Brigham and Women's Hospital in Boston. She has worked for the Harvard School of Public Health and the Veterans Administration, and for 5 years, her show "Food for Talk" aired on Boston public radio. She currently works as a nutrition consultant, helping families to improve health through diet. She has also written *Eat Well, Lose Weight While Breastfeeding* (Villard, 1992) and *Microwave Cooking for Your Baby & Child* (Villard, 1991). She lives with her family in New Hampshire.